TECHNOLOGY
ENHANCEMENT
PROGRAMME

Technology for Key Stage 3

JOHN MURRAY

Photo acknowledgements

All photos © Peter Stensel, except: cover, pp. i, 20, 26, 31, 60, 61, 62, 67, 76, 83, 114, 123, 133, 135 © John Townson/Creation; p. v © Trevor Baylis; p. 15 © Peter Shipley; p. 60 David Parker/ Science Photo Library

Papers used in this book are natural, renewable and recyclable products. They are made from wood grown in sustainable forests. The logging and manufacturing processes conform to the environmental regulations of the country of origin.

Orders: please contact Bookpoint Ltd, 130 Milton Park, Abingdon, Oxon OX14 4SB. Tel (44) 01235 827720. Fax (44) 01235 400454. Lines are open from 9.00–6.00, Monday to Saturday, with a 24-hour message answering service. You can also visit our website www.hodderheadline.co.uk and www.hoddersamplepages.co.uk

© Technology Enhancement Programme/John Cave/Bill Nicholl 2004

First published in 2004
by John Murray Publishers Ltd, a member of the Hodder Headline Group
338 Euston Road
London NW1 3BH

CD-ROM developed by Glyn Richards
Layouts by Eric Drewery
Artwork by Peter Stensel and Mike Humphries
Cover design by John Townson/Creation
Typeset in 12/14pt Eras Book by Techset
Printed and bound in Italy

A CIP catalogue record for this book is available from the British Library

ISBN 0 7195 7183 9 (single book)
ISBN 0 7195 7184 7 (Student's Book and CD-ROM)

Contents

■ Foreword

by Trevor Baylis   v

■ Introduction   vi

1 What is design and technology?   1

Design and technology starting places   4
Can your new product 'make it'?   5
Small miracles of product design   6

2 Getting ideas in and out of your head   8

Drawing   9
Advanced drawing   15
Modelling   20
Presenting your ideas   25

3 Materials   26

Properties of materials   27
Metals   29
Plastics   32
Wood and wood products   35
Smart materials   36
Getting materials into shape   38
Design and make challenges   43
Small material miracles   48

4 Structures   51

Forces and structures   52
Simple structures   54
Why some structures fall down   64
Design and make challenges   68

5 Mechanisms   70

Mechanism words   71
Mechanical parts   74
What happens next?   76
Making mechanisms   77
Design and make challenges   81
Robot challenge   85
Small mechanical miracles   92

6 Electronics in control 93

Electrons in electronics 94
Circuits 97
Switches 100
Light-emitting diodes (LEDs) 104
Resistors 107
Capacitors 112
Transistors 114
Field effect transistors (FETs) 119
Thyristors 121
Integrated circuits 124
Making a printed circuit board 129
Small miracles of electronics 130

Index 138

Foreword

by Trevor Baylis

The modern world owes a vital debt to designers and inventors. They are so often the unsung heroes whose work we take for granted when we do something as simple as opening a drink can, using a paper clip or putting up an umbrella. Someone, somewhere at sometime invented the means of doing these things, and we should celebrate the fact that design and technology in school is opening up opportunities for a new generation of young people to become creative inventors.

I have spent many years both inventing things and helping others to get ideas out of their heads, protect them, and profit from the hard work that all this entails. But the key to success is starting young – giving young people the confidence and the means to think about situations and problems, and ultimately to become the next generation of designers and inventors.

This unusual book is designed to help young people understand the search for opportunities, and provides stimulus for that indefinable kind of thinking that ends up with innovation. It is a book that I warmly support and I wish all those who dip into these pages every success!

Introduction

This book owes its origins to the work of the Technology Enhancement Programme (TEP) and the support of its publisher, John Murray. The success of the Key Stage 4 book, Technology in Practice, has led to calls for this Key Stage 3 introductory book, which is offered here with the generous endorsement of Trevor Baylis, perhaps the UK's best known inventor.

The book is unusual because, although it can be used as a conventional textbook, both the format and content offer a range of new opportunities for pupils and teachers, with case studies and challenges. Much of the content is based on TEP's Millennium Schools project which demonstrates that a high quality Key Stage 3 experience can be offered well within the financial limits of the average spend per pupil. Initial results exceeded expectations and brought a range of additional benefits for both pupils and teachers.

We live in an age of increasingly smart products and materials, and as far as possible these trends are reflected in the book in the form of real tasks that pupils can engage with. The upsurge of interest in robotics is especially noteworthy, and this important topic is covered as a means of capitalising on leisure interests within the Key Stage 3 age group.

TEP has been responsible for many curriculum innovations and many are presented here in book form for the first time. The CD-ROM (available packaged with the book: ISBN 0 7195 7184 7) serves to extend the explanatory power of words and pictures and to represent some things that would be impossible by any other means. The CD icon that appears in the book refers to relevant animations on the CD-ROM.

Single copies of the book without the CD-ROM are also available (ISBN 0 7195 7183 9).

For further information on TEP please visit: www.tep.org.uk

To obtain all the resources and materials mentioned in this book please visit: www.mutr.co.uk or contact:
Middlesex University Teaching Resources Ltd., Unit 10, The IO Centre, Lea Road, Waltham Cross, Hertfordshire, EN9 1AS. Tel 01992 716052. Fax 01992 719474.

1 What is design and technology?

Design and technology is about the things made by people and how they go about designing and making them. Studying this subject will enable you to understand objects from the past, and understand products in the present – how they work and why they look like they do. Design and technology will also enable you to become a designer and maker of things. This book will give you some guidance.

When you look around, the world is full of things that have been designed and made. When you get up in the morning, you probably take for granted brushing your teeth, putting your clothes on, looking at your watch, eating a meal. Have you ever thought about where all the things you need and want come from?

You can hardly do anything without coming into contact with things that have been designed. Designers think about what people need and use, and come up with ideas for products. No two products are the same because designers come up with different ideas. They are always trying to make things work better and look better.

■ No mobile phone is quite like another

Q How do mobile phones differ?

Many of the things you use, such as watches, radios and pens, have come about because of advances in science. Plastics and modern electronic components, such as chips, have been developed in laboratories. An electric toothbrush with its plastic bristles and rechargeable battery would be impossible without science.

When appliances, such as calculators and computers, get more powerful, we talk about advances in technology. So many products these days depend on technology.

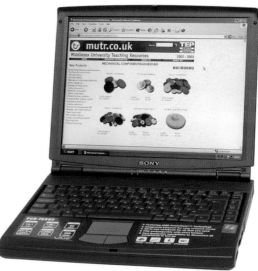

People have been designing and making things for thousands of years. In many towns and cities, you cannot dig a hole without finding something (or parts of something) that were made in the past. These things tell us a lot about people, the way they lived, and the things they enjoyed. They also tell us a lot about past technology and materials. The Victorians had telephones, but not radios as we know them. Nobody before the 1950s used plastic washing-up bowls. Early rock stars recorded on 78 rpm disks, which you now usually only see in museums!

■ Music recording has advanced from vinyl record, to tape to CD, and is still advancing…

Q If we dug a hole in a rubbish dump, we would probably find some of the following objects. How old do you think they could be?

■ aluminium saucepan

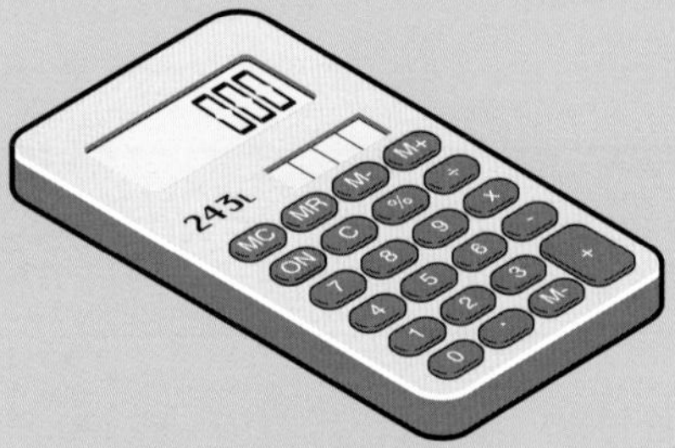

■ electronic calculator

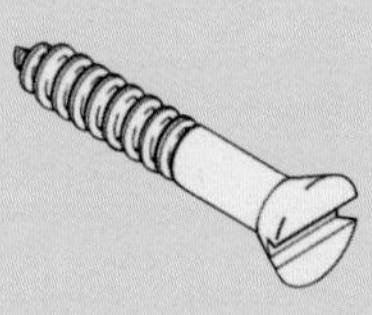

■ brass screw

■ PC keyboard

■ glass bottle

■ light bulb

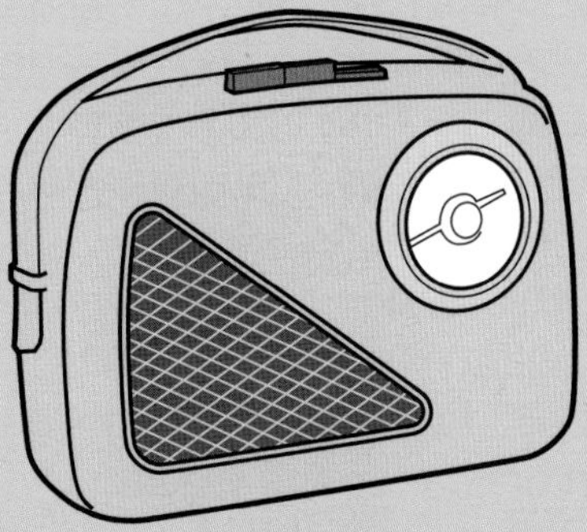

■ transistor radio

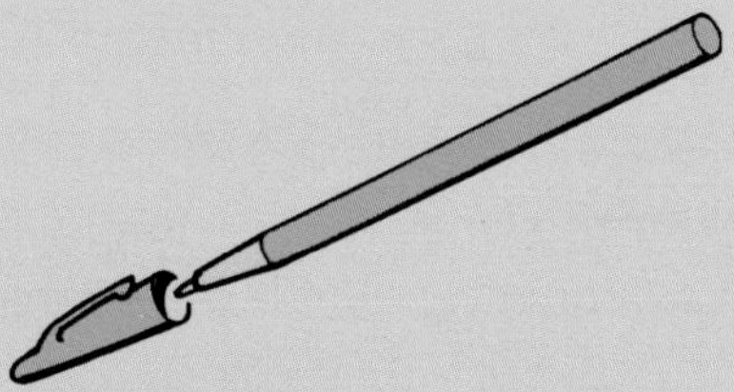

■ ball-point pen

■ pottery jug

■ photograph in frame

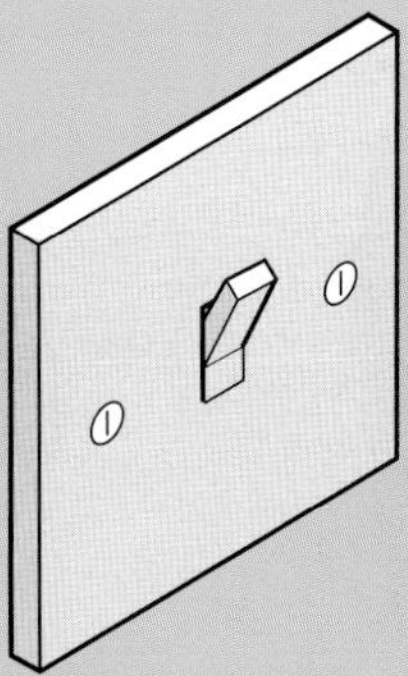

■ light switch

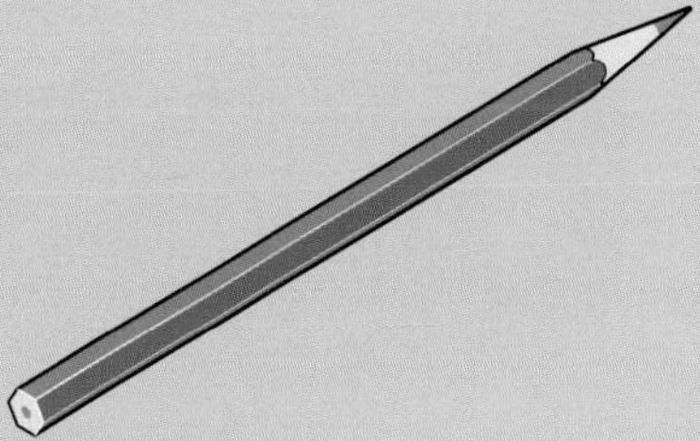

■ pencil

■ An idea for the desk clock

Design and technology starting places

■ A set brief

Very often designers are given a task by someone (usually called the client). The task is known as a brief and it sets out what is wanted. The brief might be very short, for example:

> *Design an unusual desk clock that uses a quartz movement and printed coloured card as the main body material.*

This kind of brief gives a designer lots of room for imagination. However, it does state what kind of 'works' the clock has and the main material. Since the material is card, the designer will need to work out a way of folding/joining the card to make a 3D shape.

■ Spotting a problem or opportunity

Sometimes a design opportunity will show up because someone is having a problem. Trevor Baylis, who wrote the Foreword to this book, saw a problem with the use of radios in less economically developed countries: batteries were not readily available. It occurred to him that a radio could be powered with a clockwork-driven generator. Many radios (and other products) are now clockwork driven.

In design and technology you may either be given a brief or may be asked to come up with one. If you are given a brief, you must think carefully about all the 'must do' 'must use' parts of it and then do some research. If, for example, you are asked to design a method of displaying watches in a shop window using clear acrylic, you need to find out about acrylic and look at some actual jeweller's shops. Looking in the shop windows will tell you how watches are currently displayed and may well give you ideas about how it can be done better.

It is harder if you are asked to come up with a design brief yourself. By looking around, you might be able to spot a new design opportunity. This can be very difficult. An easier starting point is to look at things that already exist, to see if you can improve them or change the way they work. An example would be the problem that older people have in using ordinary things, such as turning taps on and off.

■ Trevor Baylis's clockwork radio

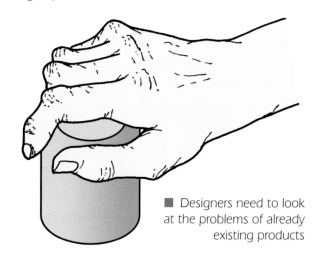

■ Designers need to look at the problems of already existing products

Can your new product 'make it'?

In looking at existing products you might ask questions like these to help you come up with your own design brief:

How well does it do the job?
Can people use it easily?
Is the product safe to use?
Is the material from which it is made suitable?
Is the product environmentally friendly?
Can the product be recycled? Is it bio-degradable?
Can people afford the product?
Do people want the product?

Products that didn't 'make it'

The answer to the last question in the list is quite a difficult one to answer because people might not know what they want until they see it!

Q Here are some examples of patent designs that did not get further than the drawing board. Can you give any reasons why they didn't 'make it'?

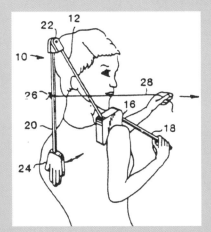

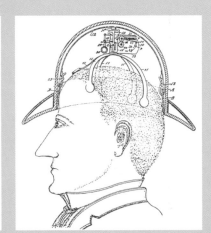

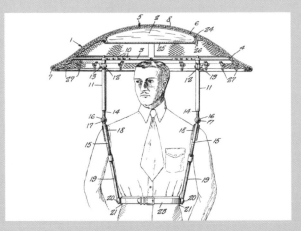
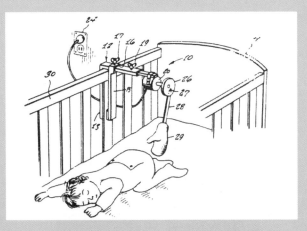

The American inventor Thomas Edison said that invention was 1% inspiration and 99% perspiration. He meant that you have to work very hard to develop an idea.

Small miracles of product design

Some products are very clever and have become successful because of the way they look and the way they work. Unlike the examples on the previous page, here are some products that have 'made it'.

Clockwork radio The clockwork radio shown on page 4 was invented by Trevor Baylis to help less economically developed countries. The original has now become smaller, and other makes of clockwork radio are common.

Ball-point pen Since it first appeared in 1938, the ball-point pen has gone on to sell billions and is now made in all shapes and sizes.

Q What other types of pen are now available?

Durabeam torch Until a few years ago most torches were simple containers for batteries with a bulb at one end. The design of the flip-top **Durabeam** torch changed all that. Since this was designed, light-emitting diodes (LEDs) and smaller batteries have given designers much more freedom.

■ Durabeam torch

Polypropylene New materials have enabled designers' dreams to come true. Many products now use polypropylene – including products that fold from a flat sheet, such as the document folders shown below.

Clockwork toys Not all popular products have an obvious use! There has been a revival of interest in clockwork, and not just for radios. You can now buy a wide range of clockwork 'designer toys'.

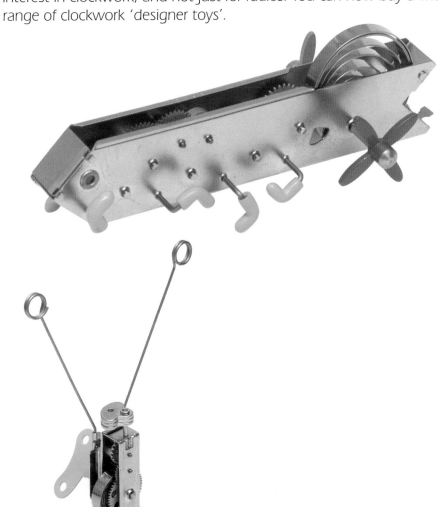

■ This toy uses a spinning unbalanced mass; it jumps around

Q Can you design a new toy with an unbalanced mass on an electric motor?

2 Getting ideas in and out of your head

Once you have a design brief, it can be quite difficult to get started. Some designers look to nature (and nature books) for design inspiration. This is an excellent starting place, for example, for jewellery. For other products, you might need to do research by looking for information in libraries or on the internet.

■ Researching the internet for design ideas

It is very important to look at actual products in shop windows and exhibitions. You will not be expected to come up with something completely different. Success is often just making a small improvement on something that already exists.

If you think about a problem, you might get an idea or two buzzing around in your head. But ideas are no good locked up there. You need to show other people what you're thinking and produce something that you can play around with and improve.

Designers use many ways of getting ideas out of their heads. They draw on paper, use a computer or, for example, make models.

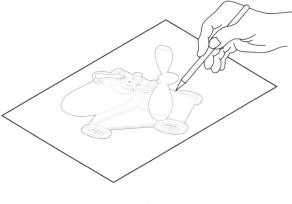

How does it work?
What is it made of?
What does it look like?
product
How could it be improved?
What are the good things about it?
How much does it cost?

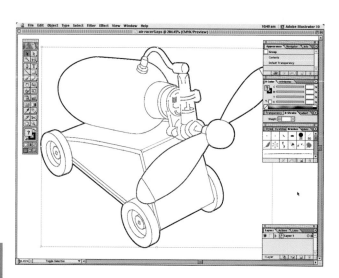

Drawing

You have an idea for something, so how do you make a picture of it on paper? If you think you can't draw, don't worry! Many of the most famous designers and inventors were not very good at drawing. Never be afraid or embarrassed to make marks on paper.

Many great inventors and designers have confessed 'I can't draw!'.

Starting flat

The simplest form of drawing is a flat outline. You can use a pencil, marker or pen. This is what most people do when they start drawing, and the outline can tell you quite a lot about an idea.

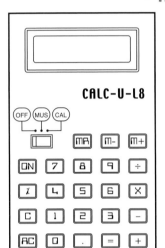

e x e r c i s e

1 Try drawing the front of your calculator. You will be able to draw something that others will recognise, like this one.

You will have learnt a lesson here: drawings have to mean something. If somebody else (or you later on) recognises the object in the drawing, then you have succeeded. Important designs sometimes start off as outline drawings. People often talk about 'back-of-envelope sketches' because when they have an idea they sometimes only have scraps of paper to draw on. It doesn't matter, as long as you get it out of your head and can understand it later on.

You can go a long way with flat outline drawings. If you want to show more than one side of what you see or have in mind, then you can draw front, side and end views. Providing these are labelled, they will give more information about your idea/object. For example, the calculator you drew in Exercise 1 might be very thin, so a side or end view would show this. Later on, you will see that this type of drawing is widely used.

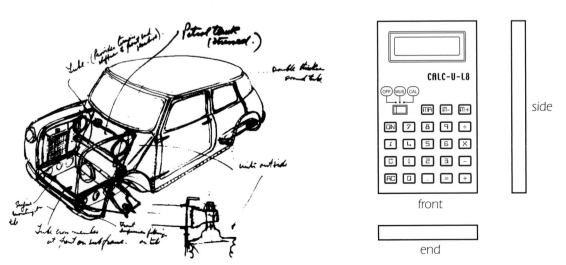

■ Sketching an idea is the first part of design

■ Making it look real

Flat drawings are an easy way to start with, but you will probably want your drawings to look like the real thing on paper. This is not too difficult, but you need to follow some rules. One method of drawing is called two-point perspective. It works like this:

1 First draw a vertical line. This will be the corner of the object nearest to you. Then mark two points (the vanishing points) on the edge of the paper above the first line.

2 Draw feint lines from the first line to these points.

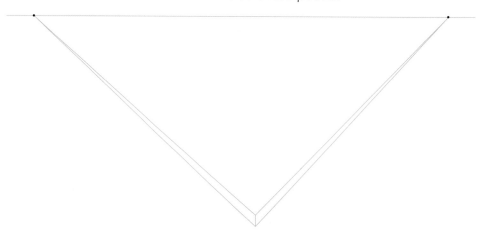

3 Draw two more vertical lines as the other corners of the object.

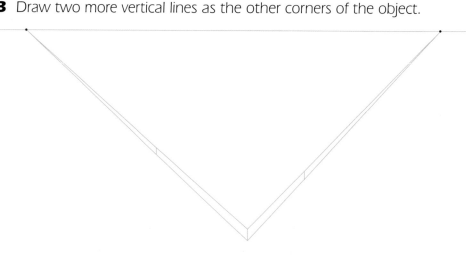

4 Now draw feint lines connecting the corner tops to the vanishing points.

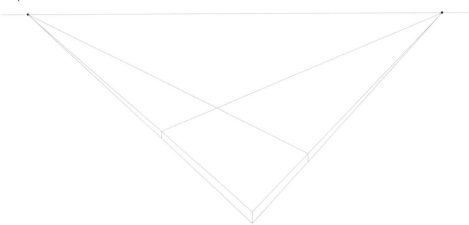

We now have a rectangle that looks 'real'. You can see at once the side, end and front, but just like looking at a real object, the side, end and top views appear smaller the further away they are. This is called perspective. This kind of outline is called a crate.

5 You can add more lines and thicken the final ones to complete a calculator drawing.

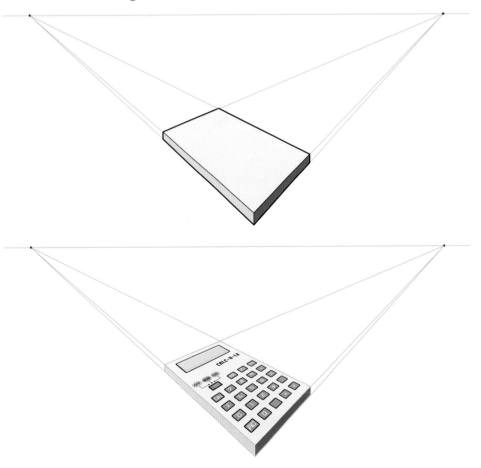

But how do you know where to put the vanishing points and the other lines? There are rules for getting this **exactly** right, but for sketching you will quickly be able to make a good guess.

Many objects are not simply made up of straight lines. There are usually curves as well. These are more difficult, but you follow the same method by drawing straight lines to form a box or a crate, which will guide you when drawing the curves.

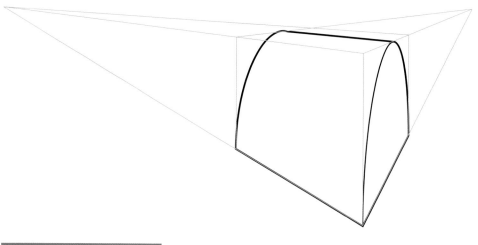

exercises

2 Make flat drawings of your calculator, showing different views, using just lines.

3 Make a perspective drawing of the same calculator.

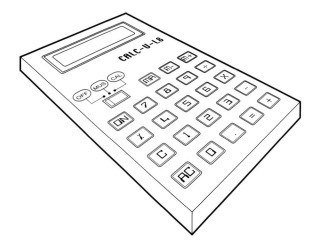

tip

✱ You can make your drawings look more interesting and realistic by using thicker lines for the outline and thinner lines for anything within the outline.

■ Shading

So far you have made an outline sketch, but it probably does not look solid. The next step is to use shading. The easiest way of doing this is to imagine that the object is lit up and some areas are in the shade – hence the name shading. If you lightly fill these areas in with a pencil, the object will start to look more solid.

exercise

4 If you want to practise, try copying and shading simple shapes like those shown below.

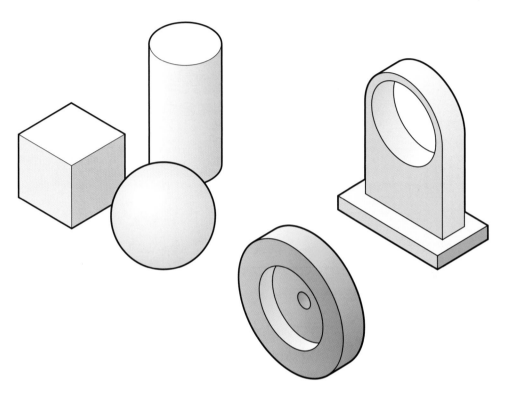

■ Colouring

Colour is a key part of our lives. You probably have a favourite colour and it might influence the things you buy. Understanding about colour can help you make important decisions. The colour 'mood' table given here will help you to choose colours to give the right impression.

Colours can be shown on your designs by carefully using crayons or felt-tip markers. If you are designing on a computer, there is a wide colour palette to choose from.

Red	energising
Orange	stimulating
Yellow	uplifting
Green	relaxing
Blue	soothing
Turquoise	refreshing
Violet	calming
White	peaceful
Black	protecting
Brown	stability

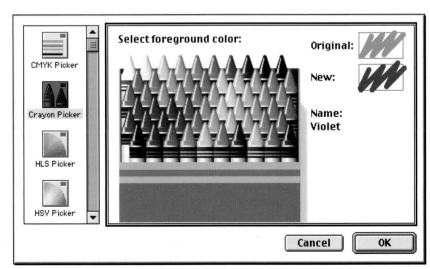

■ Annotation

Although it is said that one picture is worth a thousand words, there are times when you might need to add words to explain something. This is called annotation. You normally keep the words away from the sketch or picture by using thin lines or arrows. The words might explain, for example, what a material is or how something is supposed to move.

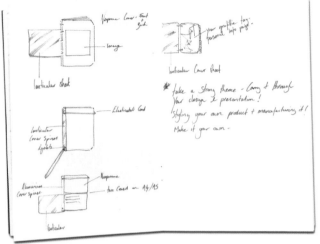

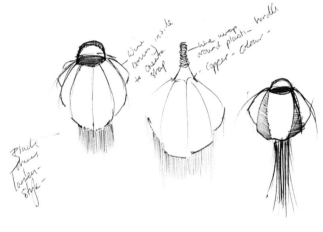

tip

* Scruffy writing on a sketch may spoil it. If your writing is a bit shaky, try printing or writing on top of a ruler. This will keep the words in a straight line and give the lettering a bit of interest when the ruler is taken away.

■ Feeling good about your sketches

After some practice, you should feel happier about drawing things to show others. If a flat outline drawing will do, then fine. If you want it to be more realistic then always try a perspective sketch. Do the box or crate outline first and then fill in with pencil. If it looks wrong, make a correction. If you can't get it right at first, leave it alone or get help. But remember: as you do more drawings, they will get better, not worse!

Advanced drawing

Marker rendering

Designers can give a very life-like appearance to things by using coloured markers. Unlike normal felt-tip pens, these have a wide 'square' tip. They can be used very effectively for drawing flat views. The sequence below shows the work of a professional designer colouring the outline of an electric grinder. You too can achieve good results in your own work if you follow the stages shown.

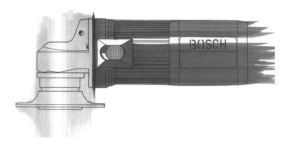

■ **1** Starting with the two-dimensional drawing, the body is streaked with a marker.

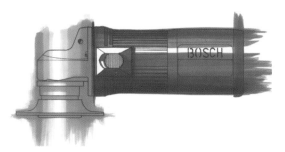

■ **2** The surface relief is shown using a darker marker or several applications of the same marker.

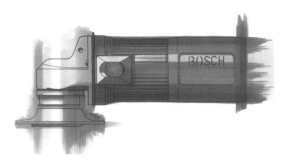

■ **3** Black and grey markers and a blue coloured pencil are used to give the appearance of a polished metal.

■ **4** A black marker is used to define the surface detail, and a white pencil may be used to show highlights where light catches the edges of a curved object.

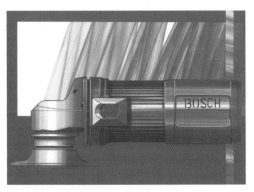

■ **5** The drawing is cut out and mounted. The example shows a backing sheet that makes the object stand out.

■ Orthographic drawings

When your design work is complete, it should be possible to make what you have in mind. Final drawings need to have detail and dimensions and be very clear. One way of doing this is to draw all the separate views of your design – looking from the top, the front and the side. This is called an orthographic drawing. If you are using pencil and paper, you can get the three views to line up by drawing feint lines across from one to the other as shown in the example.

■ Development of an orthographic drawing to show three views

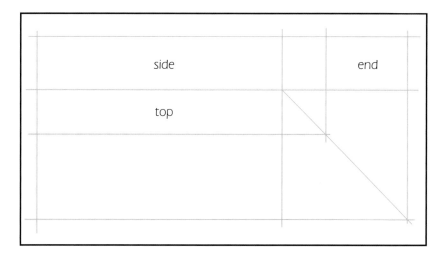

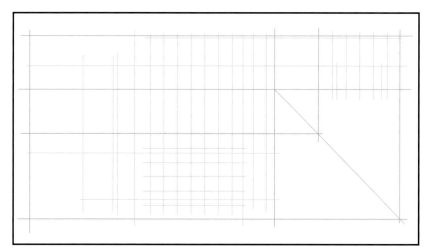

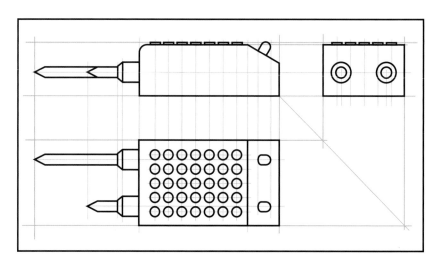

■ Using a computer for drawing

Computers cannot take over from you as a designer, but they can be useful in several ways. Computer-aided design (CAD for short) lets you draw things on screen and helps you to imagine what an object will look like. Designs that you have drawn on screen can either be printed out or the information they contain can be fed into machines to make the objects. Some computer software will let you into a 'virtual' world where you can animate what you have designed.

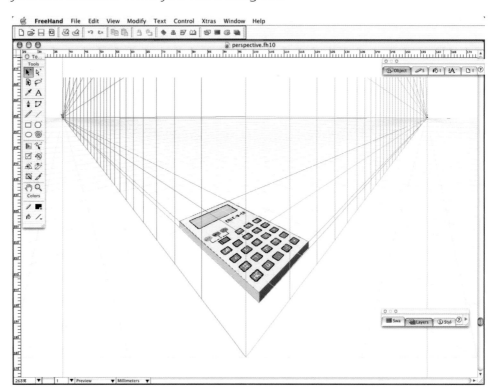

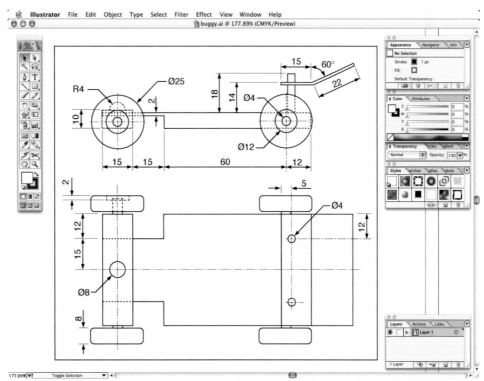

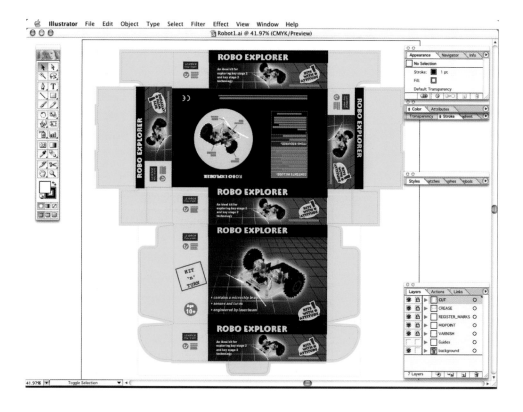

You can start designing on a computer by practising with a drawing package, such as **Corel Draw**. For this, you use the mouse and select instructions from pull-down menus. The next few pictures are screen shots which show a drawing taking shape. You should be able to pick up the techniques in a few minutes.

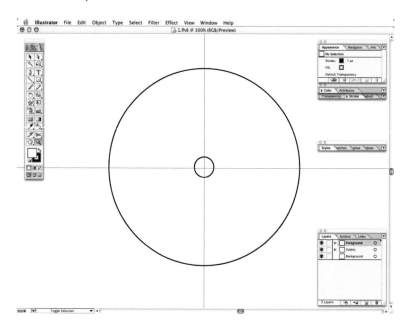

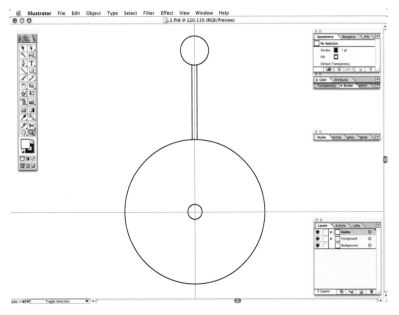

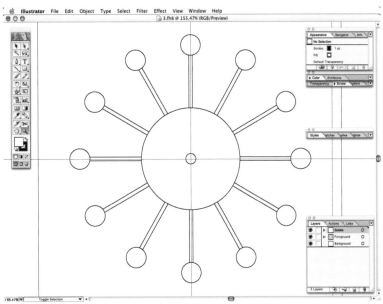

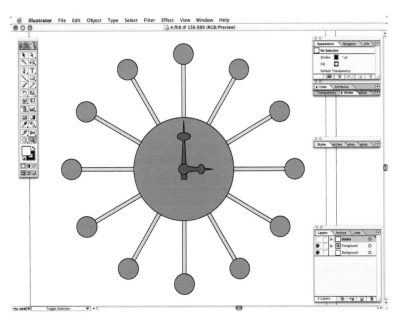

■ Modelling

As well as drawing to work out your ideas, designers also make models. James Dyson made over 5000 models before he got his vacuum cleaner right! Models that help you think and show your ideas to others can be very rough or just like the real thing, depending on what you want to 'say' or work out.

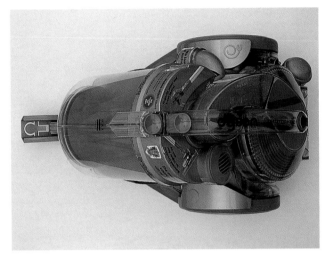

Top view

Side view

■ Rough shape models

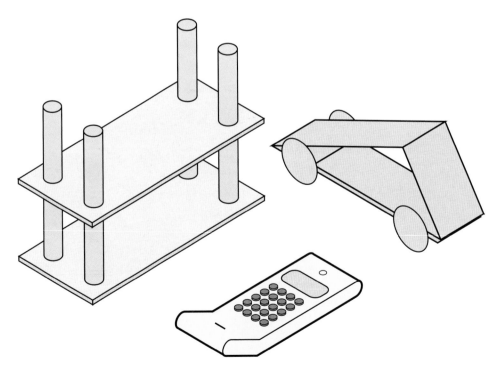

These models are made quickly to try something out – the overall look or feel, or whether they actually work.

Rough models can use almost any material to hand and very quick cutting and fastening methods. For example, you could think about using the following:

Materials: scrap card, polymorph plastic (this plastic moulds in the hand after heating in water), paper, straws, wire, foamboard, Plasticine, wooden dowels, elastic bands, etc.

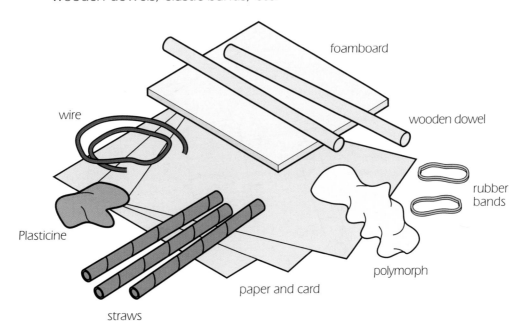

Fastening methods: Sellotape, masking tape, hot-melt glue, Blue Tac, paper fasteners, corri-joiners, etc.

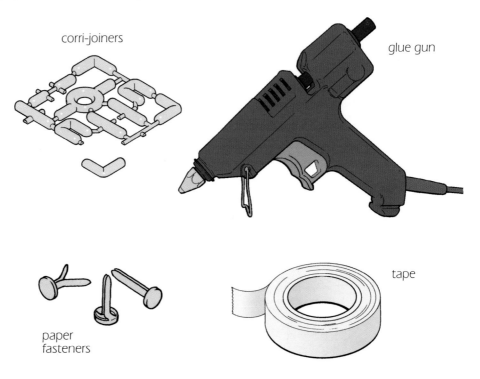

Q What other methods of joining materials can you think of? Make a list.

■ Working models

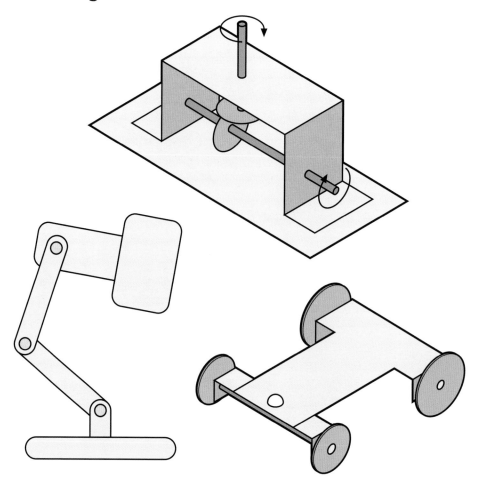

These models are made to try things out that need moving parts – like an automaton model. They can often be made from construction sets such as Lego or Meccano, but other materials and objects can also be used. For example, you can make flat mechanical models using card pieces and paper fasteners.

Working models might need electrical or electronic parts. These can be put together quickly using special prototyping boards (see page 99). The component legs are just plugged in.

■ Final models or prototypes

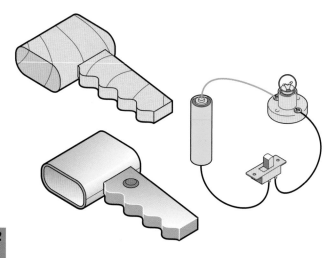

Sometimes, the best way of presenting your final idea is by making a model to look like the real thing. For example, if you have designed a torch that fits neatly in the hand, you might carve the torch body from wood and then paint it to make the whole thing look like plastic. Going one step further, you might build in an electric circuit so the torch can be tried out.

It is worth remembering that designers spend vast sums of money on final models to make sure everything looks and works correctly.

■ Using a computer for making models

Computers now drive special machines that make things. This is called computer-aided machining (CAM for short).

Machines that cut out materials are still called by their original name – CNC machines. 'CNC' stands for computer numerically controlled – a bit of a mouthful! A CNC lathe turns out circular shapes; a CNC milling machine cuts around a piece of material to leave either a flat or a 3D shape.

■ CNC machine

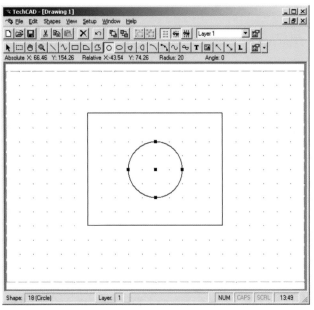

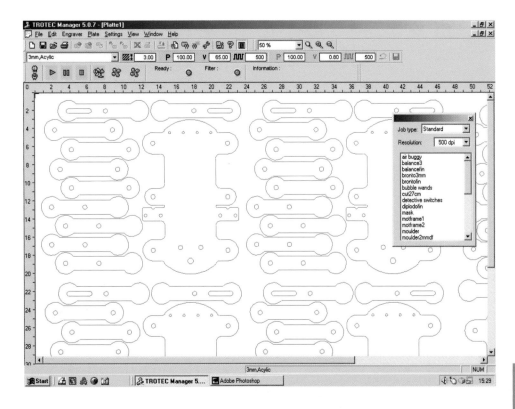

Computers are now also used to drive laser cutting machines (see page 43). A very thin laser beam moves over a surface and cuts by vaporising the material. These machines are fast and accurate, and because the cutting beam is concentrated light, the material to be cut doesn't need to be clamped.

Rapid prototyping machines – RP for short – build material up instead of removing it. These work in different ways. For example, one type of RP machine squirts liquid plastic from a very fine nozzle – a bit like icing a cake. The computer controls the nozzle to scan backwards and forwards over a surface to build up a shape. After each scan, the nozzle rises up a small amount and starts scanning again. RP machines can make shapes that it would be impossible to make by other machines.

■ **Prodigy** – a rapid prototyping machine

■ Complicated shapes like these can be built up using RP

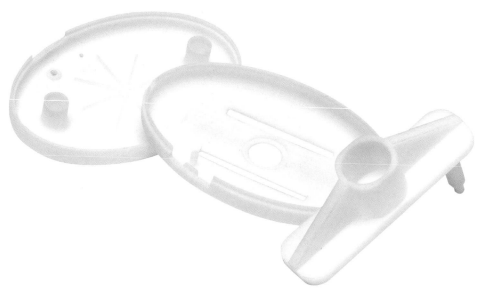

Presenting your ideas

Designers need to show and explain their ideas to other people. This means you should keep a record of all that you have done – both on paper and as models – during the design process. As a rule, keep **everything**. Mount it in a notebook or as a collection of papers in a portfolio with plastic sleeves. This will tell anyone looking at it how you have thought through each problem. The notebook or portfolio might also contain actual samples of materials you might use, or things you have found that have inspired you.

At some stage, you will need to stand back from what you have done and comment on it. This is called evaluation. You should go back to your original design brief and check it to see if you have achieved the design objective. Part of this might involve asking other people what they think of your ideas. You should show them your notes/portfolio, materials and models. If you have made something, they should actually try it out.

■ Notebooks of a professional jewellery designer

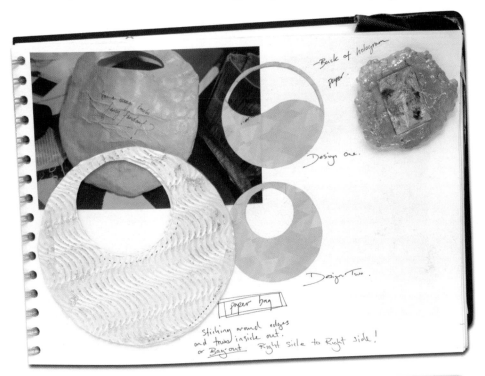

3 Materials

Almost everything we do brings us into contact with different materials. Because there are so many, we divide them into basic groups:

- metals
- plastics
- wood (and wood products)

- glass
- ceramics
- minerals (and concrete)

Note that paper and cardboard might also be used as materials (see page 21), but because they are not very strong, they are usually only used for modelling to try out ideas.

Some materials in these groups are smart. This means they react to changes in their surroundings. An example is a plastic film whose colour changes when it warms up.

- Smart film

Cold film

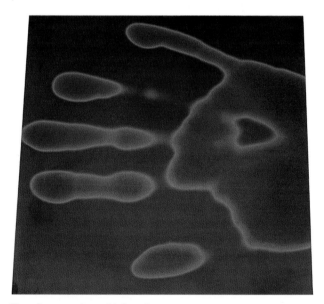

Film after pressing with hand

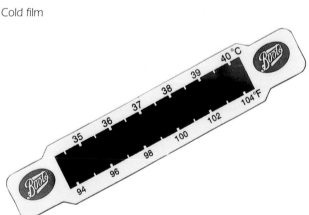

Thermometer at room temperature

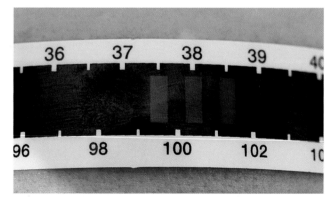

Thermometer being used to check a person's temperature

When materials from different groups are combined they are called composites. An example is plastic containing thin glass fibres – 'fibreglass' for short.

■ Properties of materials

■ Strength

Strength is an important property. You need to know if a chair will stand up to your weight, or whether the wheels of a cycle will stay circular after going over a bump. Many people think materials are either strong or weak. In fact, they are strong or weak in different ways.

A thin metal wire is strong when you hang a weight on it but weak if you stand it upright and try to make it support the same weight.

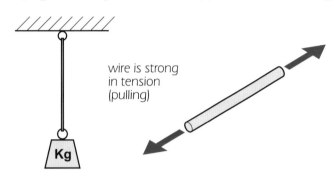

wire is strong in tension (pulling)

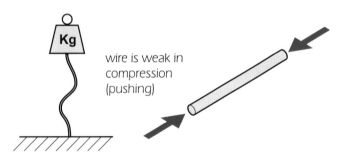

wire is weak in compression (pushing)

A piece of natural wood is very strong along the grain (both pulling and pushing) but weak across the grain. This is why well-aimed karate blows can break very thick pieces of wood.

wood is strong along the grain

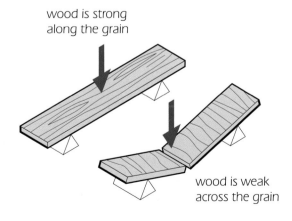

wood is weak across the grain

■ Hardness

Some materials, like polythene, are very soft. Others, like steel, are quite hard. Sometimes we need to use a soft material, like rubber in a cycle tyre. On the other hand, we usually want the ends of screwdrivers and hammers to be hard. Designers might combine hard and soft materials to make useful objects, for example in a crash helmet.

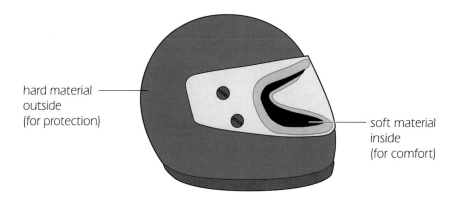

hard material outside (for protection)

soft material inside (for comfort)

■ Toughness

When you kick or hit a ball it normally has to be tough to survive. Some materials are very tough. They stand up to heavy knocks and blows. Nylon is a good example of a tough material, and it is often used in machinery. Glass, and plastics like acrylic, are not very tough. They can break or fracture easily.

■ Tennis balls are covered in nylon

Q   Why wouldn't a designer use acrylic for a suitcase or car body shell?

■ Insulation

Some materials are chosen because they are good insulators against either heat or electricity. PVC is an excellent electrical insulator and is used on electrical wires and cables. Glass, in the form of very thin fibres, is a poor conductor of heat and is used in house insulation.

Very early cables and wires used glass tubes as insulation.

Metals

■ Aluminium

Aluminium is one of the most common and most important metals. Its uses range from drink cans to aircraft wings. If mixed with other metals to form an alloy, it becomes stronger and tougher.

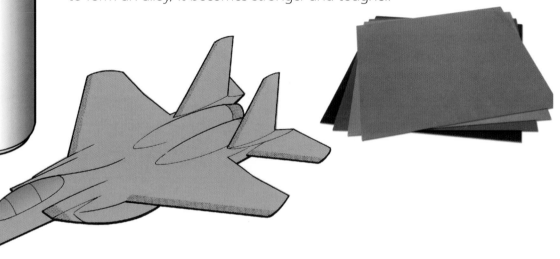

Aluminium can be coloured and protected by plastic coating or anodising. Anodising means growing a thin coat of oxide on the surface and then dying it. Most aluminium you see is protected in these ways. Sheet aluminium is sometimes plastic coated before it is shaped to save the cost of painting afterwards.

Following its discovery, aluminium was very rare for a time. It cost more than gold and was used as a precious metal.

■ Steel

This is another common and important metal because of its strength and low cost. It is a ferrous metal – one that can be attracted by a magnet. It can be mixed with other metals to form alloys, and treated with heat to give it useful properties like extra hardness or toughness.

Stainless steel contains small amounts of other metals, which cause a thin oxide film on its surface. This protects against further oxide (rust) forming. Steel is finished by painting, plastic coating or plating with other metals such as chromium. Steel is used to make car bodies.

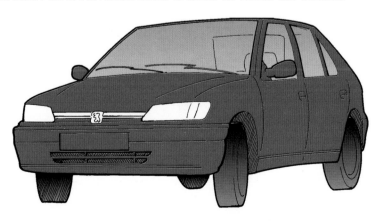

■ Silver

Silver is a precious metal used for jewellery and decorative objects. It is much cheaper than gold and you can buy small amounts for a few pence, unlike gold, which costs pounds. Over time, silver goes dull, so it is normally finished either by polishing or gold plating. A new alloy that contains germanium, however, stays shiny all the time. Silver is sometimes mixed with small amounts of copper to give it strength.

■ Silver jewellery parts

■ Copper

Copper is a non-ferrous metal – not attracted by a magnet. It is a very good conductor of electricity and heat. It is used for water pipes and in electrical wires and cables as a conductor of electricity. It is also used in the wire windings of electric motors. Copper can be polished, but it will go dull very rapidly.

■ Copper pipes

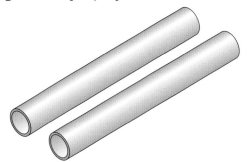

■ Brass in plug

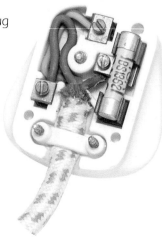

■ Brass

Brass is a mixture of copper and zinc. It is non-ferrous. Brass is a good conductor of electricity and heat and is used in electrical fittings, such as plugs.

Titanium

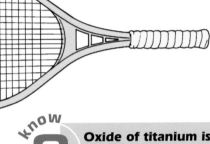

■ Titanium in frame

Titanium is a metal normally mixed with others to form an alloy. It is extremely light but at the same time very strong. Titanium is used for jewellery, for sports equipment, for components in aircraft engines and more expensive cycles. It can be coloured by anodising, but this is a slightly different process from anodising aluminium.

 Oxide of titanium is pure white and is used for brilliant white paints.

Pewter

This is almost pure tin metal. It is soft and polishes to a high shine. It is used to make ornaments and drink containers. Pewter melts at a very low temperature and can even be cast into wooden moulds.

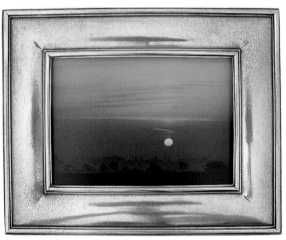

Picture frame

Hip flask

Love cup

Tankard

Old pewter contains lead and can be poisonous.

◼ Plastics

Some materials with plastic properties are natural materials, like animal horn. Most plastics, however, are manufactured in large chemical plants. Most plastics you will come across are thermoplastic. This means that they will soften when heated, and can be reshaped when soft over and over again.

◼ Acrylic

This is a hard plastic available in sheet form. It can be clear, like glass, or coloured. It is often used for making signs or small objects, like menu holders.

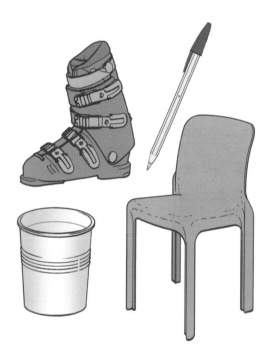

Acrylic has more names than any other plastic material: it is also called Perspex, Lucite and Plexiglass.

◼ Polythene

This is a soft plastic which is very strong in tension. Large amounts are made into thin sheets for plastic bags. It is also moulded into items such as wheels, washers and electrical insulators.

When the world-wide demand for carrier bags goes up, the price of raw polythene increases.

■ Polystyrene

Polystyrene is an inexpensive, general purpose plastic that is produced in sheet form and as mouldings. It is used widely for vacuum forming, where the heated sheet is drawn down over a former (mould). Uses range from chocolate box liners to toys.

■ Polypropylene

This is a very tough material, often made into thin sheets. You can fold it without heating and it can be flexed backwards and forwards any number of times without breaking. Polypropylene is often used as a hinge material, for example the covers for clip file binders.

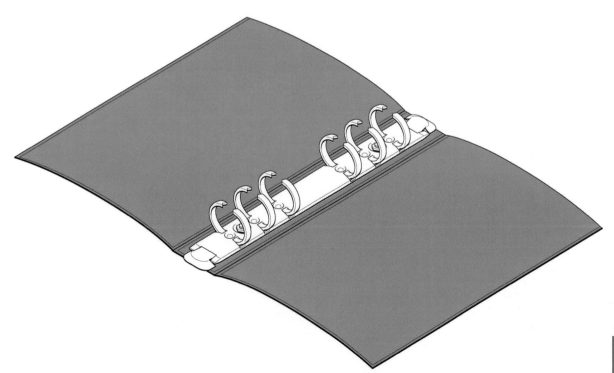

Polymorph

This is one name given to a type of plastic that softens at very low temperatures. Most plastics need heating to well over 120°C before they soften, but polymorph granules can be softened for moulding in hot water at about 62°C. Polymorph has many industrial uses, but is an ideal modelling material. You can heat it and mould it by hand. When cool, it is as strong as other plastics.

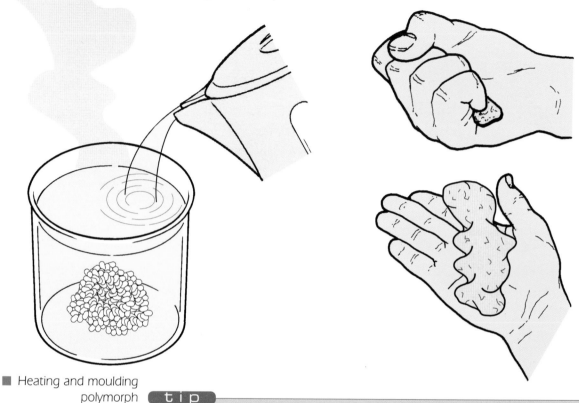

■ Heating and moulding polymorph

tip
* WARNING: Do not use boiling water. Take care handling hot polymorph.

Foamalux: TEP modelling board

This is a sheet plastic whose centre is full of small air bubbles like an Aero chocolate bar. It is extremely light, but strong. It can be cut with a sharp knife or saw. It is often used for display boards but is also an excellent model-making material.

Wood and wood products

Wood is one of the oldest and most important natural materials. In its natural form – as cut from the tree – it is used in furniture and buildings. Wood is also made into other materials, such as paper and card. It is also used to make MDF (medium-density fibreboard), chipboard and plywood.

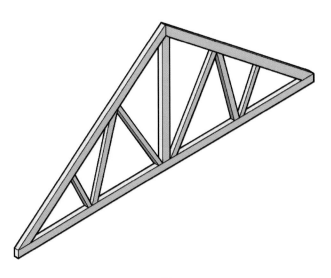

Natural wood

Wood cut straight from the tree is called 'green' wood. It contains a lot of moisture. To be of real use it has to be dried, and this may be done in a kiln. Natural wood can absorb moisture and expand or it can dry out and shrink, even when it is made into something. We see a lot of natural wood in roof frames of new houses and in furniture.

Because of the high cost of decorative woods, these are often made into thin sheets called veneers. These can be applied to large surfaces of furniture, such as tables, whose main frames are made of cheaper woods.

did you know? Wood still expands and contracts after thousands of years. Ancient Egyptian furniture has to be kept in special temperature- and moisture-controlled cases to stop any damage.

MDF (medium-density fibreboard)

MDF is a bit like very thick cardboard. It is made from wood fibres that are mixed with glue and compressed into thick sheets. MDF comes in different thicknesses and is used a lot for making furniture.

Chipboard

Chipboard is made from chips of wood that are mixed with glue and compressed into sheets. It is a very cheap material that often contains waste sawdust. It is used for floors in modern houses. It is also used in furniture where it is veneered or coated with a hard plastic called melamine.

Plywood

This is made from veneers that are glued together as layers. It is a very strong sheet material that has many uses. These include furniture making and to make moulds for casting concrete in buildings.

Smart materials

Smart materials appear to have a mind of their own. They seem to be intelligent – hence the word 'smart'. Smart materials can be based on either metals or plastics. Plastics are often combined with special chemicals to give them their smart property.

Shape memory alloy (SMA)

This is a mixture of metals, for example nickel and titanium. SMA has a memory. When you heat it up, it remembers to change to a different shape. When it cools, it goes back to the first shape. A material called smart wire (SMA wire) remembers that it should be shorter when heated. If you pass electric current through it, the wire heats up and shortens. This wire is used in mechanisms to make parts move.

■ SMA wire is used to make mechanisms

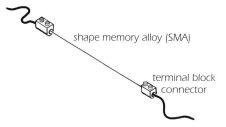

shape memory alloy (SMA)

terminal block connector

Thermochromic film

'Thermo' is to do with heat, and 'chromic' with colour. Thermochromic film changes colour when you heat it. It is a thin plastic, coated with special liquid crystals – similar to the ones used on calculator displays and flat computer screens. When these get warm, they change colour. Thermochromic film is used for stick-on thermometers and for warning patches, which show when something like a computer is getting too hot.

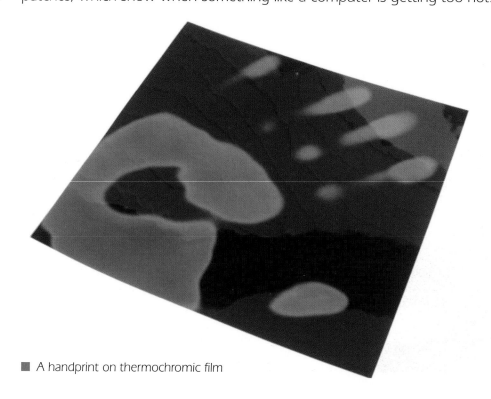

■ A handprint on thermochromic film

■ Smart colours

This is the name given to two types of material: thermochromic pigment and photochromic pigment.

Thermochromic pigment

This material changes colour when heated. It is contained in millions of tiny plastic bubbles in a paste. The paste can be mixed with acrylic paint, which will then change colour when heated. Thermochromic pigment can be mixed into plastics so that they colour when a certain temperature is reached. An example is a baby's feeding spoon.

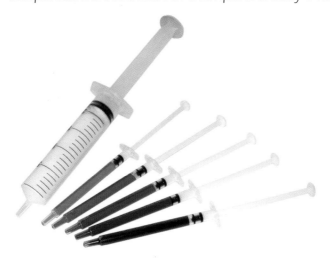

Photochromic pigment

This material changes colour when exposed to light. It is also contained in millions of tiny plastic bubbles in a paste. The paste can be mixed with acrylic paint, which will then change colour when put into sunlight. This material is used to make colour-changing notices, clothes and even nail varnish.

■ Glow-in-the-dark torch

■ Glow-in-the-dark materials

Many plastic objects glow in the dark. They are made from plastic containing a special fluorescent chemical that stores energy from light. This energy is then given out as light, which can be seen in dark places. The same chemical can be mixed with acrylic paint to produce glow-in-the-dark paints.

> **Q** Smart materials are used in clothing. Can you give any examples?

■ Getting materials into shape

You can make things with materials using hand tools and machines (called machine tools) – see **Hands-on making** below. It is now possible to drive a machine direct from a drawing on a computer screen – see **Hands-off making**.

■ A laser cutting machine is operated directly from a computer and can be programmed to cut shapes extremely accurately

■ Hands-on making

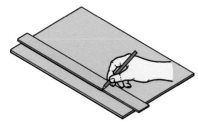

■ Marking out wood with a pencil

Unless you are using something like a laser cutter to make things, you have to mark out the work before anything else. On most materials you use similar marking out methods but slightly different tools. You draw lines on wood with a pencil, and lines on metal and some plastics with a scratching tool called a scriber. Measurements are usually made with metal rulers, and lines are drawn at 90° to each other with try-squares. For metals and plastics, we often use a flat surface to help with accurate marking out. In engineering, this is called a surface plate.

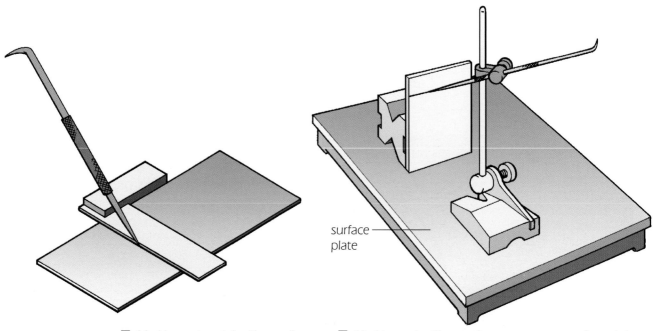

surface plate

■ Marking out metal with a scriber   ■ Marking cut with a surface gauge on a surface plate

Sheet metals

Aluminium sheet is marked out using a scriber. If the aluminium is already anodised or plastic coated, a fine spirit pen can be used.

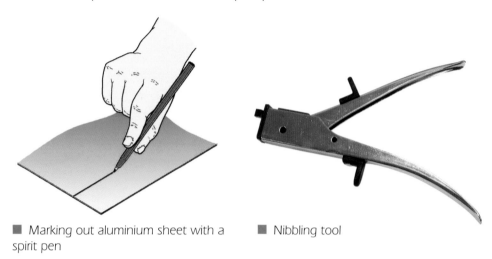

■ Marking out aluminium sheet with a spirit pen

■ Nibbling tool

14 Aluminium sheet can be cut with a special guillotine or a nibbling tool. This nibbles out small pieces of material and leaves the sheet flat. Shears can also be used but these distort the sheet.

15 Holes can be made using punch tools. The sheet can also be drilled, but this is more difficult and so more dangerous to do.

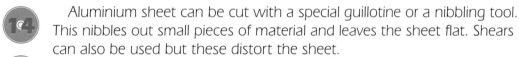
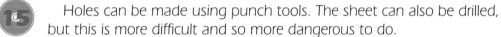

■ Punch tool

■ Folding tool

16 Aluminium sheet is bent over with a folding tool. This ensures a clean fold at the angle wanted.

17 Aluminium can be joined by screws, rivets, or double-sided adhesive tape.

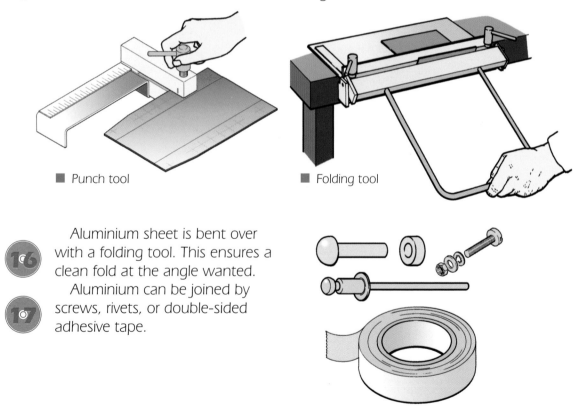

London buses and parts of aircraft are held together with adhesive tapes.

Sheet plastics

Polystyrene Polystyrene is marked out either with a pen or scriber as for wood and metals. It can be cut with a guillotine, nibbler or by scoring a line and then cracking. To do this, you make a deep scratch with a scriber or knife tool, and then break the sheet over an edge – like a table edge. Goggles must be worn to prevent splinters from getting into the eyes.

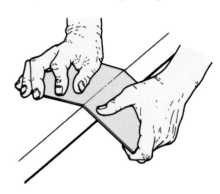

tip

* Always wear goggles when snapping poystyrene.

Holes can also be made with punch tools.

Polystyrene sheet is folded by heating along the fold line on a strip heater and then bending.

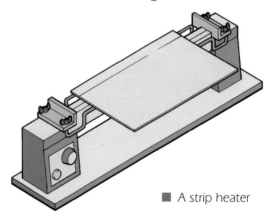

■ A strip heater

Polystyrene sheet can be fastened by special liquid adhesives. These should be used in a well-ventilated place to prevent fume inhalation. It can also be fastened using screws, rivets or double-sided adhesive tape.

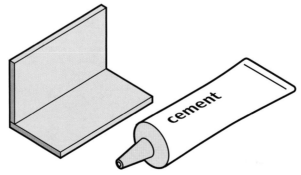

■ Polystyrene sheets joined with special adhesive

Acrylic Acrylic is marked out with a scriber or pen. It can be cut by sawing using a suitable saw. A tenon saw can be used for straight lines or a coping saw (with fine blade) for curves. The acrylic must be held firmly and cut close to where it is held.

■ Coping saw

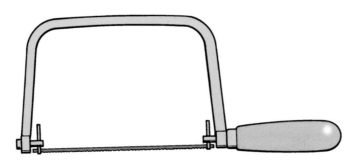

Holes are made in acrylic by drilling. A special drill is used and the work must be held tightly in a vice.

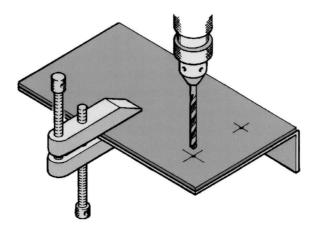

Like polystyrene, acrylic can be folded by heating along the fold line on a strip heater and then bending.

It is fastened by special liquid adhesives. Again, these should always be used in a well-ventilated place. Acrylic can also be joined using double-sided adhesive tape. Screws and rivets can also be used – they must not be done up too tightly or they will crack the acrylic.

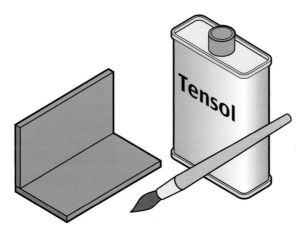

■ Acrylic pieces joined with tensol

Wood

Wood and wood products are marked out using a pencil and sometimes a knife tool. They are cut with different saws, whose shape and tooth size differ widely. For small, general work a tenon saw is used.

Holes are made by drilling.

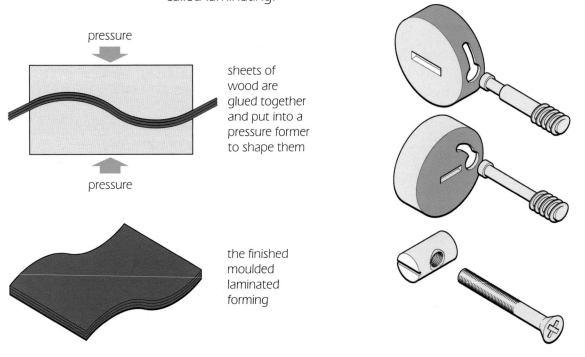

Wood cannot normally be bent into shape unless it is specially heated. Thin layers can be glued together in a mould to make curves. This is called laminating.

pressure

sheets of wood are glued together and put into a pressure former to shape them

pressure

the finished moulded laminated forming

■ Fittings and screws for woodworking joints

Wood is fastened using adhesives. PVA is the most common glue used. Natural wood is joined by fitting it together with woodworking joints, special fittings, screws and nails. Wood products such as MDF can be joined with special fittings, screws and nails.

■ Hands-off making

You can get from an idea to making a finished part using a computer-controlled machine. These are usually called CNC machines (see page 23). One type of computer-controlled machine we talked about uses a laser beam for cutting the material (see page 24). A powerful laser can cut most materials, including metals. Smaller machines used in schools can cut card, plastics and wood. You do not have to clamp the material down because the laser beam does not push against anything as it cuts.

Practically any shapes you draw on screen can be cut out of material by the laser very accurately. The size will be exactly what you key in to the computer, and the finish on the cut edge will usually be perfect. You can make things by laser cutting that are up to the standard of products sold in shops.

■ Laser-cutting

Design and make challenges

It's all done with mirrors

Many mirrors are now made from plastics with a shiny metal film. Mirror polystyrene can be cut just like ordinary sheet polystyrene and so can be turned into almost any mirror shape.

Can you design and make a mirror for personal use?

It might need other materials to make a protective case. The protection could be a fabric sleeve.

Three mirrors in a tube make a kaleidoscope. These Victorian toys have become very fashionable again and many people make a living by creating new types of kaleidoscope – especially the part that causes images to move past the end of the tube.

Can you design and make a kaleidoscope?

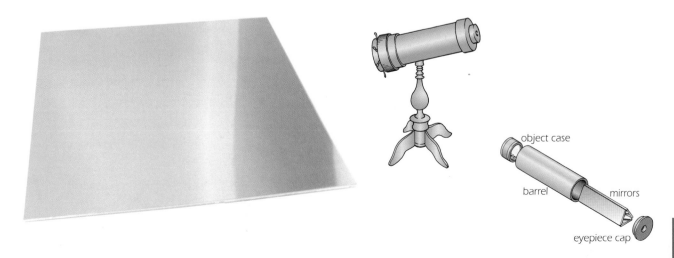

object case

barrel

mirrors

eyepiece cap

Changing mood

There is scientific evidence that aromatherapy fragrances change moods, for example, lavender relaxes. Many people just enjoy the fragrances of aromatherapy oils.

Can you design and make a device that will fill a room with fragrance?

Oils will evaporate more quickly from a surface if air is blown over it. What about a small fan inside a case? Plastics, wood or metal sheet – even all three – could be used.

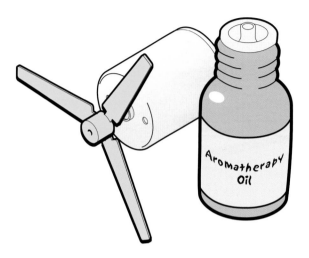

It speaks

Electronic sound modules, such as radios or voice recorders, are now very cheap.

Can you make a case for one?

The electronics mean that the case can be practically any shape – providing you can make it. Simple is better than complicated, but try to think of something unusual. Radios have been made and sold in many different forms: radio in a plastic bag, radio in a matchbox, radio in fabric container… and many more.

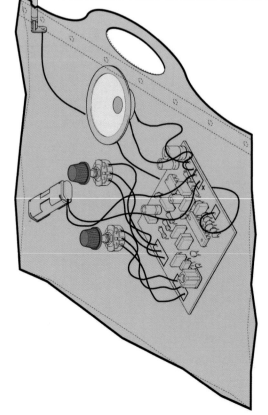

Getting organised   Personal organisers have made a comeback – that's official! After everyone thought that electronic notebooks would take over, the paper organiser is now selling more than ever before.

Can you design and make a personal organiser with a cover and flat inserts? Use the organiser spine as a starting point. Polypropylene is a possible cover material because it can be flexed without breaking. Page dividers, rulers and other flat objects can easily be made from plastics or metal sheet.

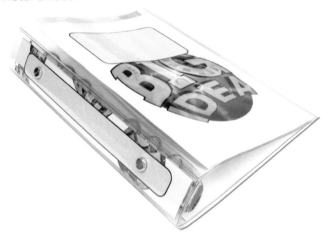

Making your mark   Printing from blocks is a very ancient craft. Marking with rubber stamps is a simple version of block printing. This process is still used for making some wallpapers and fabrics. Personal stamps are still used for marking books, writing paper, envelopes, gift-wrap paper, etc.

Can you design and make a personal stamp?

The stamp material itself can be made from cut lino, cut card, foam – anything that takes up some ink. You need to think about mounting the stamp itself and storing it, maybe in a small case. You can buy ink pads or make one using blotting paper.

Fits like a glove
People take the handles on the things they use for granted. But some handles are more comfortable and work better than others. Elderly people, and those with specials needs, might need different handles on everyday things.

Can you design and make a small product with a handle designed to fit the hand?

It might be an aid for opening ring-pull cans, or a simple screwdriver. You might consider modelling the handle with a material like Plasticine. The handle could then be made, for example, with polymorph.

Playing the game
Small pocket games are very popular. These may include noughts and crosses, draughts and chess.

Can you design and make a game with a number of similar pieces?

This challenge is to make a board and the pieces. The board might be produced as a graphics design on the computer and the pieces cut out or punched out of sheet materials.

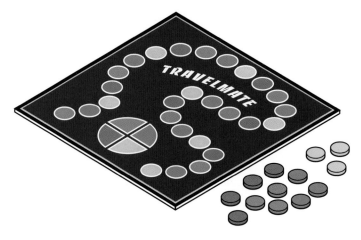

In between the covers
You may have noticed that some books have unusual bindings. Examples include:

- an art book sold in a plastic bubble
- a book on conservation bound in recycled wooden sheets
- a book on fashion bound in a fabric cover
- a journal on aeroplanes inside a metal casing.

Can you take a paperback book and make an unusual cover for it?

The new cover (back and front) might be fastened to the old covers. On the other hand, you might consider making a new flexible spine and covers that the old book will fit into.

Keeping track of it

There are many types of labels for luggage and personal goods. Some 'designer' labels are now made in coloured metals.

Can you design and make a label for a case or bag that gives it security and adds to its appearance?

Think about designer labels on clothes and bags that people go out of their way to show off.

Time flies...

Clocks offer unlimited opportunities for original design. Many famous designers have come up with new-look clocks and we see different sorts almost every day. Modern quartz movements provide the clock: can you provide the design?

Remember: plain and simple can be interesting. You do not have to use numbers arranged in a circle, and hands can be any shape.

You can stick very light materials, such as paper, onto the ordinary hands.

Thinking of you

Jewellery is big business, but a lot of modern jewellery uses low cost materials in unusual ways.

Can you design and make a piece of modern jewellery, such as a brooch?

It might use one or more materials including plastics and possibly even silver.

It becomes very easy if you use some ready made fittings like brooch backs. You can then concentrate on the real design.

■ Brooch made from found objects

Small material miracles

One hundred years ago, before modern plastics and metal alloys, designers had very little choice about what materials they could use. Now a designer is spoilt for choice and new materials can themselves be designed to order. Modern living would be impossible without the materials we now take for granted. For example, clocks can be made from practically any material ranging from paper to painted metals. This is why designers can always create something original, despite the thousands that already exist.

Aluminium Most drink cans are made from very thin aluminium. The same material is used to make aircraft and power lines.

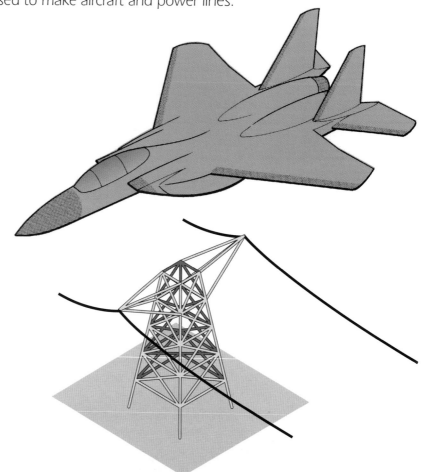

The most sheet aluminium used in the home is in the kitchen – as aluminium baking foil.

Polypropylene Polypropylene is used to make a wide range of fold-up goods because it can be flexed so easily without breaking. One unusual example is a fold-up coat hanger.

Titanium Titanium is used in jewellery as well as aircraft engines. Many fashion-conscious people prefer titanium jewellery to gold because of the colours.

■ Titanium in aircraft

■ Titanium brooch

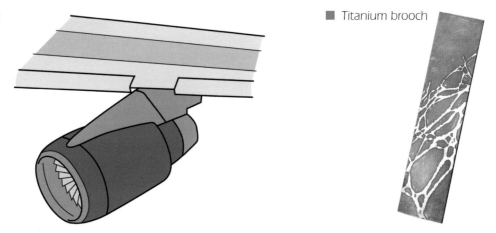

Wood Weight for weight, wood can be stronger than steel. It is still used for some very large structures, such as building frames, instead of steel.

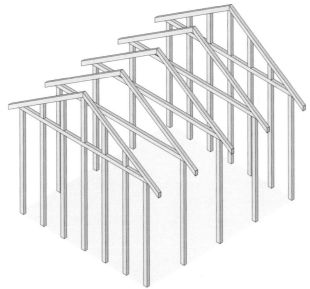

did you know?

Wood was still used as the main building material in Second World War aircraft. Only some aircraft, such as the Spitfire, were made from metal.

Acrylic You will probably have seen acrylic in shop signs, but you might not know that it is used to carry light and information in optical fibres. When light enters one end of an optical fibre, it bounces off the sides until it reaches the other end – this can be for up to several miles. Acrylic is also used to carry light to different places in a product such as a calculator.

■ Optical fibre

Silver Silver is used to make precious objects and jewellery. If silver is stamped with a hallmark, this guarantees its purity.

Thousands of tons of silver per year go into the making of photographic films.

4 Structures

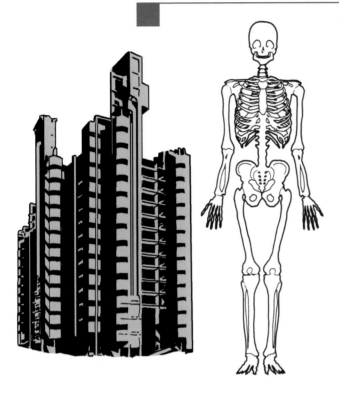

When people think of structures, they probably think about bridges or buildings. But there are many other kinds of structure, ranging from the human skeleton to packages in a supermarket. One thing they have in common is offering support of some kind.

Our own skeleton has evolved over millions of years as an incredibly strong frame. This supports all our soft tissues that make up most of our mass – most of which is water. We see many other structures in nature, such as plant stems. These have developed as hollow tubes for stiffness.

Almost everything we buy in a supermarket is sold in a structure called a package. Packages contain and protect their contents, and allow them to be stored and moved without damage. They may be made from cleverly shaped card, plastics or even metal.

Drink cans are incredibly strong even though the metal is thinner than some paper.

 Just ten empty drink cans standing upright can support the weight of a car.

Forces and structures

Structures stand up to forces that try to change their shape. There are three main forces, each with a special name.

Compressive force

compression → [   ] ← compression

When a structure is squashed or squeezed we say that it is being compressed or is 'in compression'. An everyday example would be the legs of a chair. When you sit down, your weight squashes the legs between the seat and floor.

Tensile force

tension ← [   ] → tension

When a structure is pulled apart or stretched, we say that it is in tension and that the forces are 'tensile'. An everyday example would be a plastic fizzy drink bottle. The pressure inside keeps the thin walls in tension, a bit like a football. Unlike a ball, though, the bottle is designed as a structure to keep its shape and stand up on the shelf.

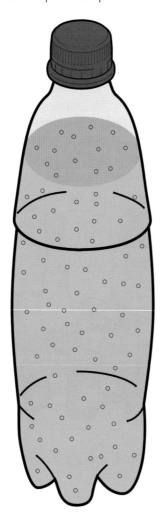

■ Shear force

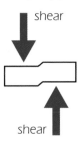

shear

shear

An everyday example of a shear force is cutting paper or card with scissors. The paper or card is sheared where the blades come together. We say 'the material is in shear'. Shear forces act on parts of many structures. For example, the pins that hold up shelves in kitchen cabinets or bookshelves are in shear. If a pin is too weak, it will break. Sometimes parts called shear pins are built into machines as a kind of safety valve. They break and stop the machine before any real damage is done.

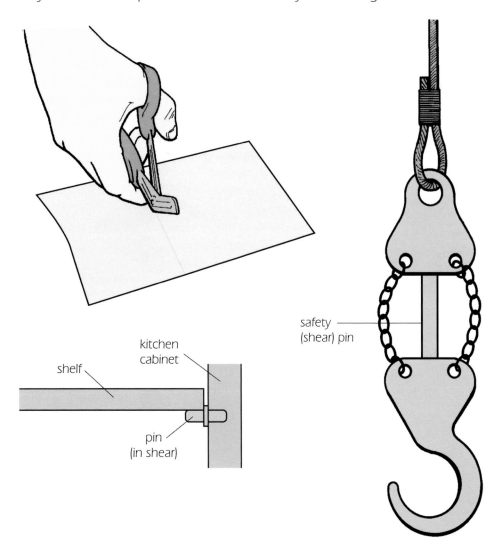

kitchen
cabinet

shelf

pin
(in shear)

safety
(shear) pin

In most structures different forces are acting at the same time. You must know about these to understand how a structure 'works' and to make it work better. Luckily we can do this by making paper models of important structures that behave just like the real thing.

■ Simple structures

■ Beams

■ Beam bridge

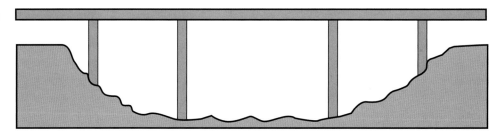

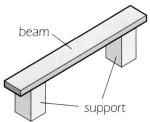

beam

support

Beams are important parts of larger structures such as bridges or buildings. They span across a gap to support a structure like a floor. Designers try to make beams as stiff as possible, so they don't sag. They also try to make them very light so that they don't sag under their own weight. One way of doing this is to use sheet material. This is normally quite 'floppy' but if folded the right way can become stiff and support far more than its own weight.

e x e r c i s e s

1 Take a piece of paper and lay it between two books. It will bend in the middle, even under its own weight. This is not a very good example of how to make a shelf. Have you seen shelving that sags badly under the heavy weight of things such as books?

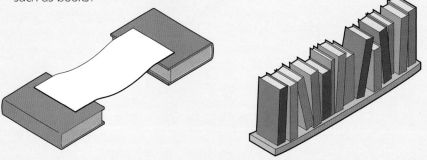

2 What happens if you now fold the paper into a concertina shape?

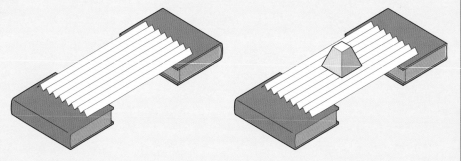

It becomes much stiffer as a beam. Not only will it support its own weight, you can place other masses on it and it will support those as well. You have turned a 'floppy' material into a stiff beam.

Steel and aluminium sheeting is folded like this to make stiff but lightweight parts for much bigger structures. Examples include supports over windows in buildings, roofing and parts for aircraft.

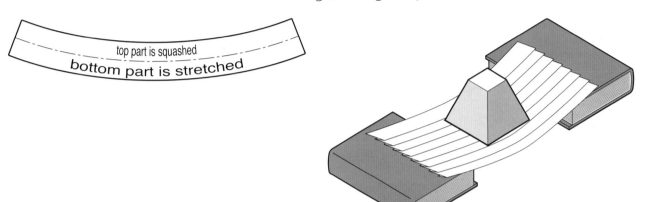

top part is squashed

bottom part is stretched

So, what forces are acting on the beam you have modelled from paper? If you think about it carefully, there are two different forces at work: compression (squashing) and tension (pulling). The top of the folded paper beam is compressed and the bottom is being stretched. If you put a much bigger mass on the beam, it will fail. Try this out and see what happens. The beam will crumple at the top as the folds move sideways. If you can stop the folds moving sideways, the beam will be much stronger. The easiest way of doing this is to glue sheets of paper top and bottom. You will then end up with a very stiff but lightweight structure, like corrugated cardboard.

Structures made up from thin materials are used widely in things ranging from doors to aircraft parts, but they all 'work' in similar ways.

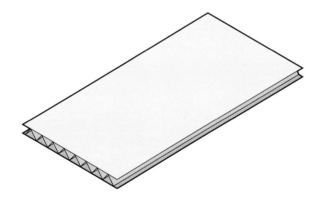

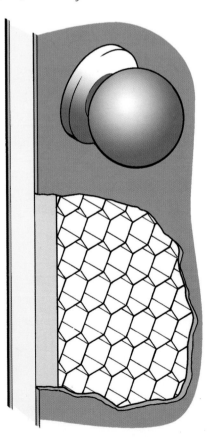

■ Boxes

Another way of making a beam is to fold the paper into a square tube and tape along the side. This is called a box beam.

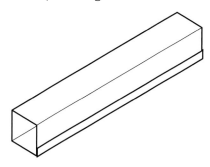

3 Fold a piece of paper into a box beam with sides of roughly 20 mm. Lay it across a gap. Test how much weight it will support.

It will support its own weight without sagging and will also support small masses.

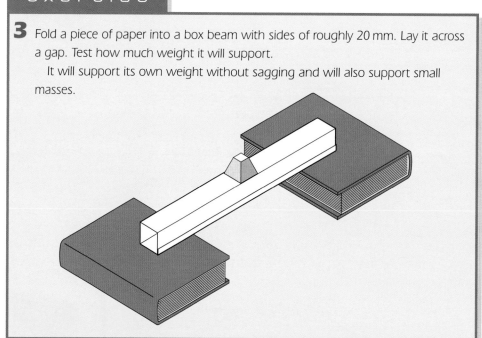

The sides of the box beam 'work' like the concertina beam. The top part is compressed and the bottom part is stretched. When the box beam fails, it will probably fall over sideways and go flat rather than crumple at the top. Preventing this from happening will make the box beam stronger. How can you do it?

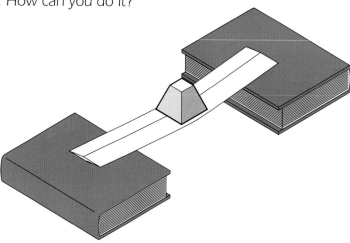

■ Failed box beam

One way is to thicken the walls of the beam. Another way is to glue a length of material inside. A third way is to glue small squares inside. These are called webs.

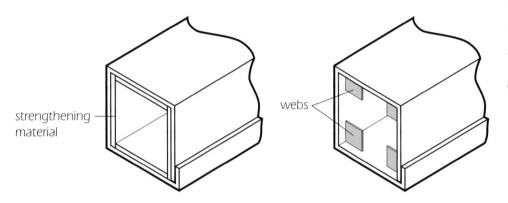

strengthening material

webs

When a beam becomes a box

If you think about it, a very short beam will become much stronger if you attach just two webs – one at each end. These stop the tube from folding over flat. And this is just what box and package makers do when they make a package that is to contain something.

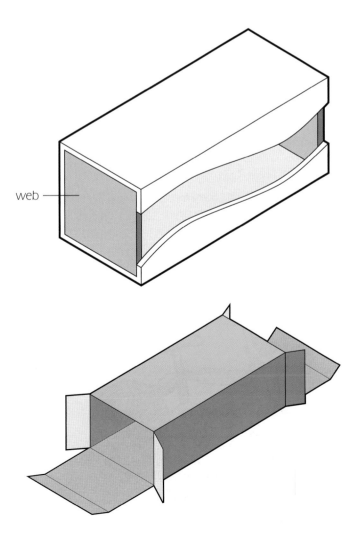

web

4 Find a card package with two tuck-in ends – like a toothpaste box. **Without** the ends tucked in, place it across a gap and put a mass on top. Eventually the box folds over flat. Now tuck in the ends and see the difference. The box should stand up to a much larger weight.

Where is the strongest place on the box? If you put it on a flat surface and press down, you will find it is at the corners, where the two sides and ends come together.

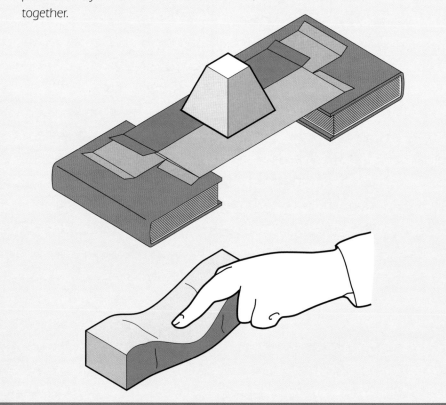

■ Frames

A frame structure uses a number of smaller parts joined together. A cycle frame is a familiar example. Other examples are less obvious, but very important. The supporting structure for a house roof uses a number of frames called trusses. These are made as strong as possible to support heavy tiles. To reduce cost, they also use the least amount of material.

5 You can model frame structures by making parts from rolled paper. These are called roll tubes. Follow the steps to make the tubes:

- Glue along one edge of a roll of paper with stick glue.
- Roll the paper around a special roll tube mandrel. This has a slot to insert the flat paper.
- Slide the paper tube off the mandrel.

The tubes can be cut to length and each end flattened and punched to allow easy joining to other tubes.

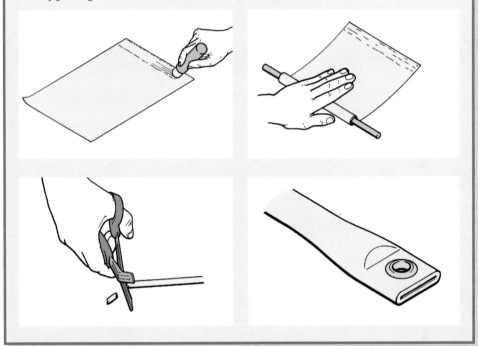

Very simple and strong frame structures are based on triangles. If you make up a simple square frame with roll tubes or parts of a construction set, it can be pushed over at an angle. If you now make a triangle, this cannot be pushed around so easily. To get the best of both worlds, you can add a diagonal part to the square frame.

A triangular frame that stands up by itself can be made from just six roll tubes.

can be pushed over

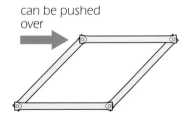

cannot be pushed over

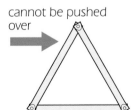

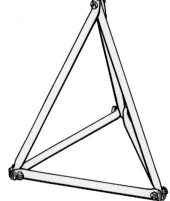

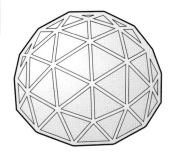

■ Geodesic frames

A famous designer and inventor called Buckminster Fuller created special frames that he called geodesic. These are now used in many buildings, such as the dome of the Eden Project in Cornwall and the roof of the Great Court in the British Museum. Models of these structures can be made using roll tubes and special plastic joiners. If you have an idea for a geodesic building or structure, you can easily make a model of it and test it for strength.

■ Dome of the Eden Project

■ Roof of the Great Court in the British Museum

Part of roof

Close up of frame

know did you

Carbon can be made to form into minute geodesic spheres less than a millionth of a metre across. They are called 'Buckyballs' after Buckminster Fuller.

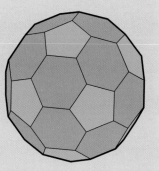

■ Buckyball

■ Structures with wires and cables

Some structures make use of stretched wires or cables. A good example is the London Eye, which uses massive cables to create a structure like a giant cycle wheel. A cycle wheel works in exactly the same way. When all the spokes are stretched (in tension), the rim is pulled towards the centre of the wheel and becomes a very stiff ring.

■ The London Eye

Front view

Side view

Cables attached to hub

Cables attached to rim

■ Cycle wheel

Other large structures that use cables are bridges. These can be suspension bridges or cable-stay bridges. Both use very thick cables to hold up the bridge deck to span long distances.

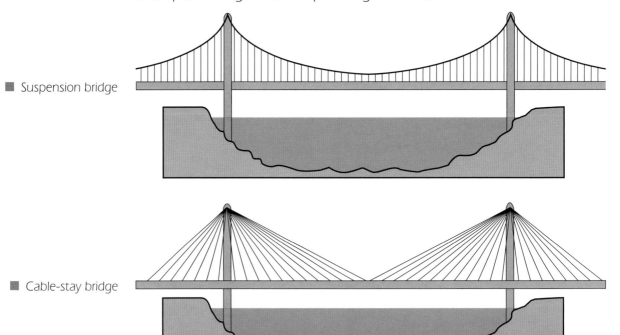

■ Suspension bridge

■ Cable-stay bridge

Many hi-tech buildings now use cables as part of their structure. The most famous recent building is the Millennium Dome.

■ The Millennium Dome uses cables as support

Side view

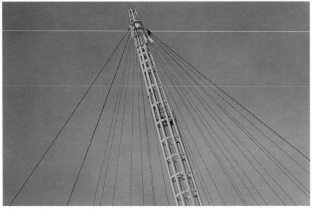

Cables attached to pylon

Cables attached to roof

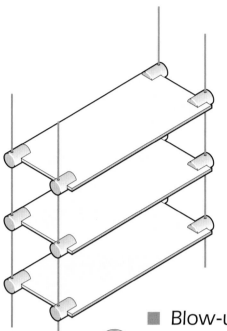

Smaller examples of structures that use wires (and cords) include fold-down furniture such as shelving and storage units. Storage units sometimes use fabrics in place of wires and cords.

■ Blow-up structures

25

Blow-up structures include chairs, boats and even complete buildings. When a flexible tube (or other shape) is sealed and filled with air it expands as far as it can and goes hard, like a balloon, games ball or cushion. Large structures such as bouncy castles are made from several tubes and shapes all connected together and stiffened by pumping in air. Some structures, such as chairs, are pumped up once and then sealed. Others like bouncy castles and some buildings are pumped up with a continuous supply of air from a fan.

You can model inflatable structures using thin polythene bag material seamed with adhesive tape. Even quite large structures made in this way can be inflated by a small battery-powered electric motor and propeller.

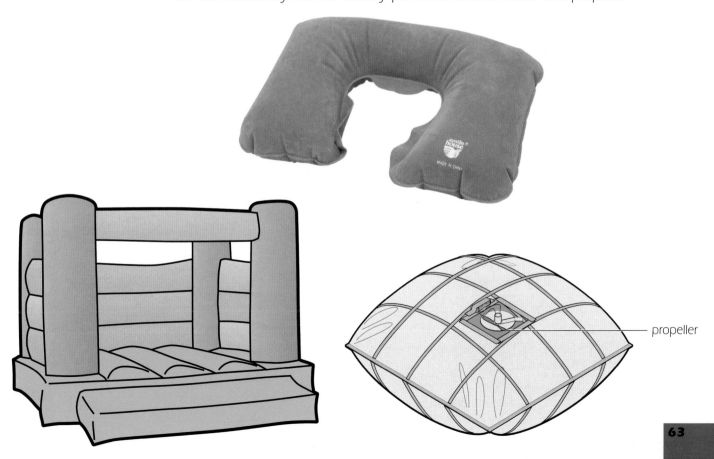

propeller

Why some structures fall down

Designers of structures do not always get it right. Sometimes you see goods in a supermarket that are damaged because the container is too weak – very often this happens at the corners. Sometimes a building, bridge or other structure collapses because of a design fault. Here are some examples.

Building collapse

The hi-tech interior of a modern building in America had a number of walkways suspended one above the other. All of a sudden they collapsed, and a number of people died. It was quickly realised that the suspension joints at the top were only strong enough to hold one walkway, not all of the additional walkways below. One of the top joints failed in shear, leading to the accident.

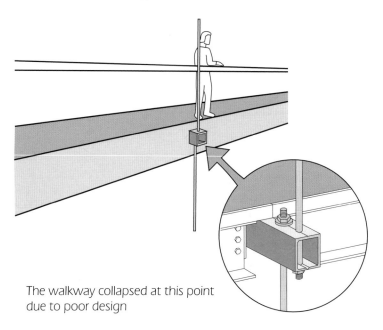

The walkway collapsed at this point due to poor design

Aircraft failure

The first commercial jet aircraft had a serious structural fault. Several crashed before it was realised there was a tiny area of weakness near a window. When the aircraft was pressurised in flight, the outer skin was stretched. When it landed, it relaxed again. After several flights, the skin suddenly tore open, just as a balloon will burst from a tiny hole made by a pin.

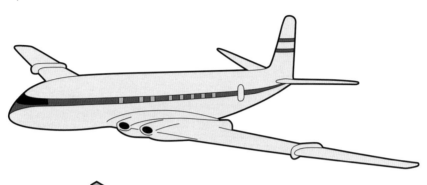

Shelf and roof failure

You may have noticed that some roofs and shelves sag in the middle. This is because of something called creep. This happens when a material gradually deforms over a long period of time. Eventually, the sagging part may break. It can be prevented by choosing the right type and size of material.

did you know ?

Some ships have broken in half in rough seas. This is because a hull can tear like paper if there is a tiny weakness such as a small crack. You can try this with paper. If you try to break a strip of paper by pulling, it is very difficult. If you try again after making a small nick in the strip, it tears easily.

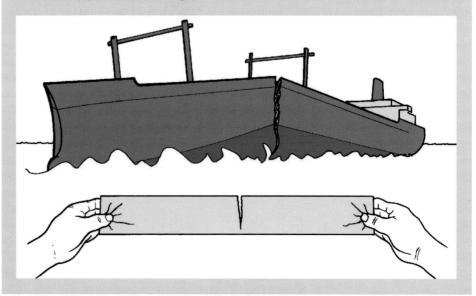

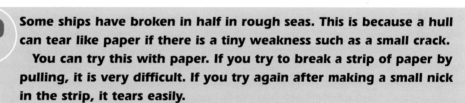

■ Preventing problems before they happen

Designers must think carefully about structures at the design stage to avoid failures later on.

Q Look back at the examples of ideas at the rough design stage on page 5. Can you spot any more problems now? If so, what improvements would you make?

Q A customer complains that supermarket trolleys are too small and suggests extending the length. Do you think this will work?

Q A DIY enthusiast makes up a bookcase by screwing four shelves between two uprights. Will it do the job?

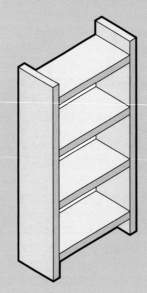

The Millennium Bridge over the Thames is a very unusual structure supported by steel cables running along the sides. When it was opened, it wobbled so much from side to side as people walked on it that the bridge had to be closed for a year while engineers designed and fitted special dampers.

Side view

Cables

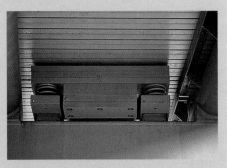

Damper under deck

Damper above deck

Design and make challenges

Special packaging When books are transported, they are often dented at the corners. This is called 'bumping' and it costs the book trade a lot of money to replace damaged stock. Using only a single sheet of thin card, design a package that can be used to send a small paperback book safely through the post.

Paper frames Many smart 'designer' products use recycled materials such as paper. Using roll tubes, design a table-top frame for displaying photos. This might be supplied in kit form so you can think of unusual and colourful ways of joining the roll tubes together.

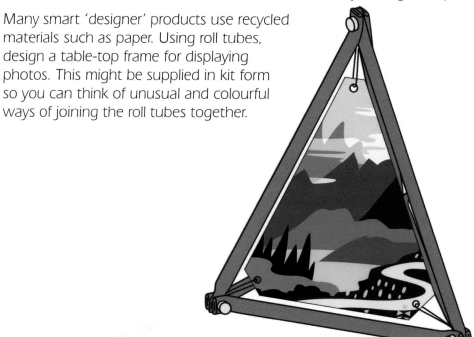

Geodesic frames Geodesic frames can be a cheap solution to temporary plastic-covered buildings. Design and make a model of a geodesic frame for a small greenhouse. Make roll tubes for the frame parts. If you do not have any plastic joiners like the one shown, try using folded wire, pipe cleaners or star-shaped joiners cut out of card or soft plastic containers.

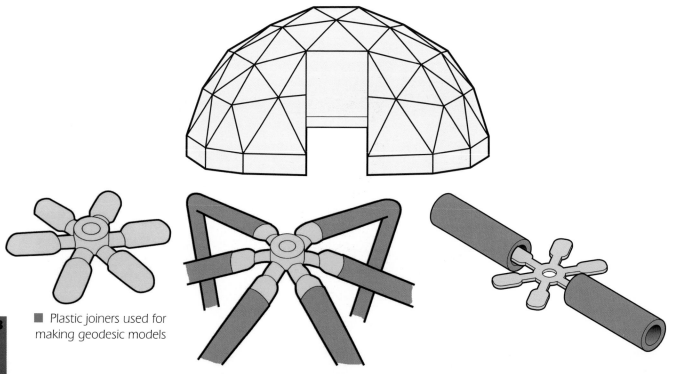

■ Plastic joiners used for making geodesic models

Hanging structures

Hanging furniture is a popular and inexpensive solution for storage. Design an interesting and colourful hanging storage unit for books or small objects of your choice. It might use some stiff materials with wires, cords or fabric. Your unit might be made as a model or a full-size working unit.

■ Hanging shelves

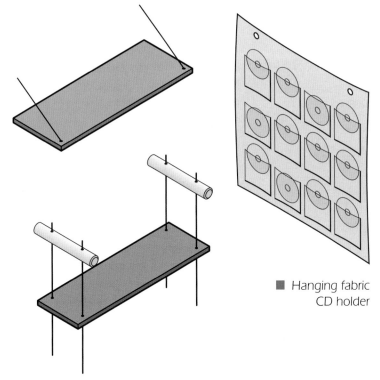

■ Hanging fabric
CD holder

Inflatable structures

Inflatable structures are quite eye-catching, so they are often used for advertising. Design and make an inflatable shape to advertise an event or product in a place such as a shopping centre. Remember that a small propeller (150 mm across) driven by a small battery-powered electric motor will provide enough air to keep a structure of up to 1 m³ inflated.

tip

＊ WARNING: Take care with any plastic sheeting. Improper use can lead to suffocation.

5 Mechanisms

We are surrounded by mechanisms, and use many every day. When you put a CD into a player, use a cycle or just turn a door handle you will be using a mechanism. A car contains many mechanisms, including the engine and gearbox.

A mechanism is two or more moving parts connected together. A turning door handle is connected to a sliding part that keeps the door shut. The pedals on a cycle are connected to the rear wheel by a chain drive. The engine of a car is connected to the wheels via a number of gears.

Although some mechanisms can be very complicated, they are made up from just a few parts that are easy to understand. Once you understand how these work, you can put them together to make your own model mechanisms. Some of the problems you might have had in understanding how things work might now be solved. This is because making models first allows you to make a few mistakes.

■ A drawer in a CD player

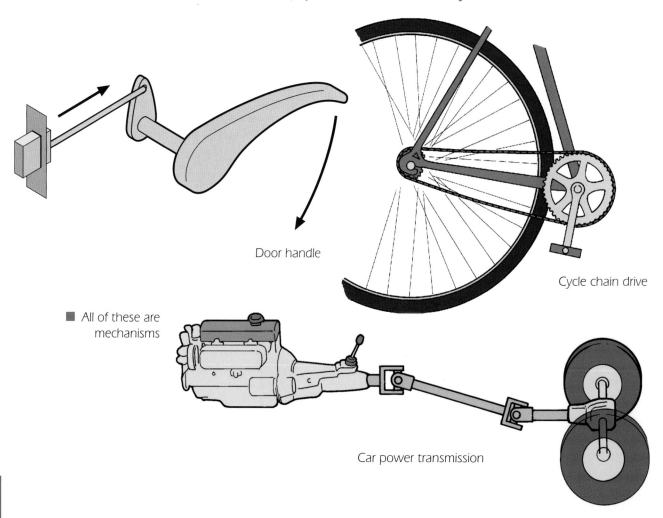

Door handle

Cycle chain drive

■ All of these are mechanisms

Car power transmission

Mechanism words

Cam A cam is a specially shaped wheel. When it turns, something resting on it – called a cam follower – moves.

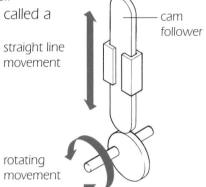

straight line movement

cam follower

rotating movement

Crank A crank turns rotating movement into straight line movement. It can also work the other way, for example, when the piston of a motorcycle engine turns a crank.

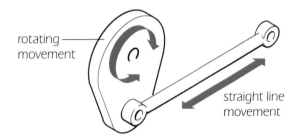

rotating movement

straight line movement

Gear Gears are toothed wheels that **mesh** (connect) together and drive one another around. They can increase or reduce speed, and change the direction of something that is turning. Some gears are shown here.

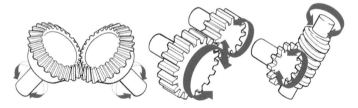

arrows show movement

Gearbox A gearbox is a collection of gears meshing together. Sometimes an electric motor is attached – this called a motorised gearbox.

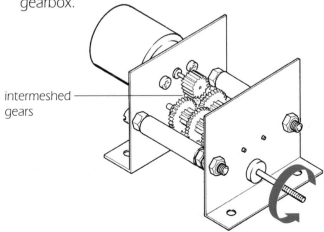

intermeshed gears

Lever   A lever is something that moves about a pivot. If the pivot is in the right place, you can move a big load with quite a small effort.

■ This type of lever could be used for lifting or moving heavy objects, or prising lids off cans

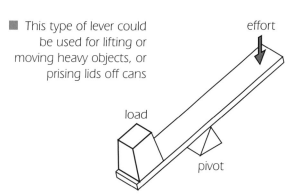

■ This type of lever is used in wheelbarrows – the pivot is the wheel

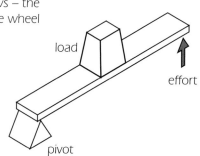

Linkage   A linkage is something that moves from 'A' to 'B'. Linkages can be made from rods, strips of plastic or just card. Some linkages are shown here.

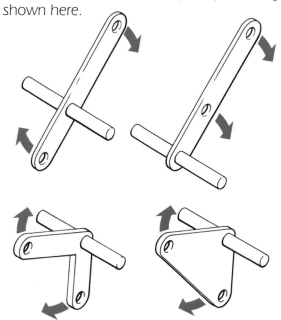

arrows show how the mechanism can move

Pulley   Pulleys are grooved wheels connected by a belt. They can increase or decrease speed.

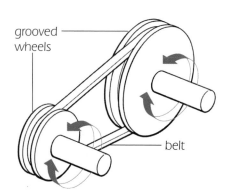

Smart grease (also called motion control gel)   This is a 'sticky' grease. It has the same effect on mechanisms as sauce around a bottle top. It slows things down but gives a very smooth feel to the movement of the mechanism, such as this camcorder cassette door.

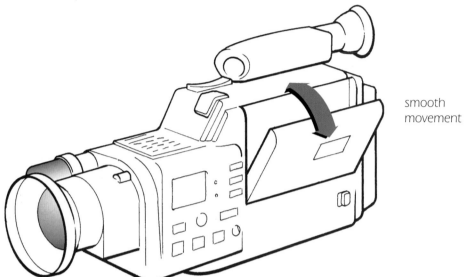

smooth movement

Softlink tubing (sometimes called smartlink)   Softlink tubing enables you to join mechanical parts, and change the direction of something that turns. Because it is soft, it allows you to change the movement.

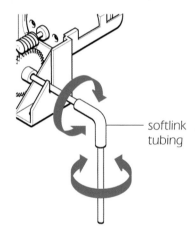

softlink tubing

arows show possible movement

Spring   A spring stores energy. It can be stretched (pulled) or compressed (pushed in) and will try to return to its original length.

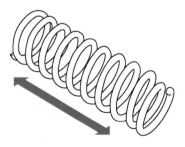

Q How many things can you think of that use springs?
Make a list and say what each spring is used for.

■ Mechanical parts

  Some of the parts used in mechanisms, like gears, are quite difficult to make. Instead, these can be bought quite cheaply.

The gears and cams are made from polythene and have a 3 mm hole in the centre that fits tightly onto a shaft.

Gearboxes can also be difficult to make, but there are a number of ready-made ones to use with an electric motor already attached.

■ Ready-made gearboxes
with motors

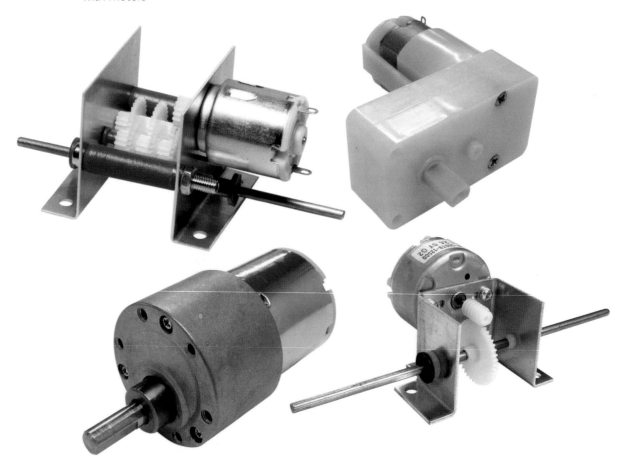

Coiled springs are also available in many shapes and sizes, but you can have fun making these by winding wire around a mandrel. A pencil can sometimes be used in place of a mandrel. Flat springs can simply be made from naturally springy sheet like polypropylene.

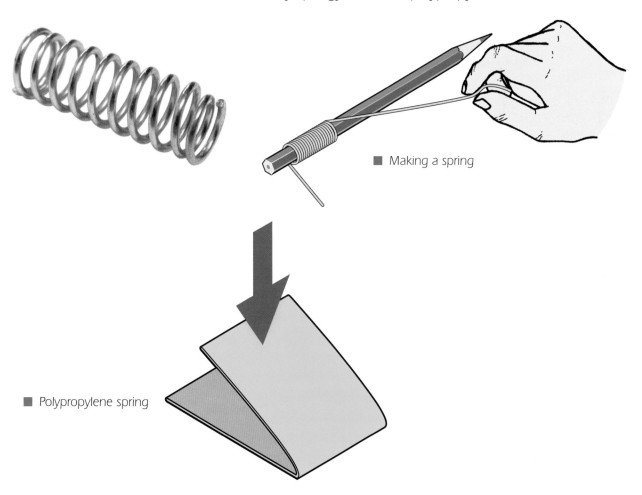

■ Making a spring

■ Polypropylene spring

Linkages can be made from flat materials like card or plastic or metal sheet and joined, for example, with screws and nuts, rivets or eyelets. Aluminium rod can be used with these flat materials to make links. It is easily bent and can be held in place with short lengths of softlink or other plastic tubing (see pages 73 and 80).

Cranks can be made from flat materials, or by connecting other parts. A plastic cam or wheel plus an aluminium rod will make a simple crank mechanism.

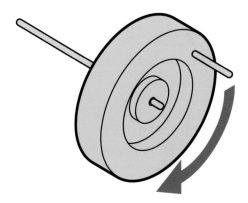

■ What happens next?

Q Several years ago scientists developed tests to try and find out if some people were better at understanding mechanisms than others. In their tests, you had to predict what the mechanisms would do. Can you provide the answers?

DESCRIPTION OF TESTS

(a) Explain what would happen if the tap C were turned on and left.

(b) What is H for?

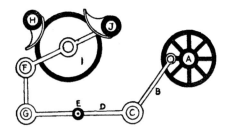

Diagram 3.

(a) What happens to I if A is turned clockwise?

(b) If A's direction of turning were reversed, would it affect I's movement? If so, how?

(c) If E were removed, would it affect the working of the machine? If so, how?

(d) What is J for?

(e) Why is J this shape?

(f) What is H for?

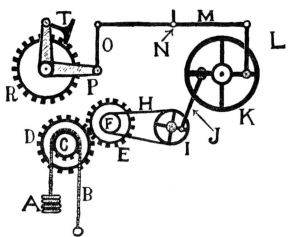

Diagram 4.

(a) When B is let go, what happens to R?

(b) When B is let go, what happens to K?

Making mechanisms

Construction kits

You can make some mechanisms using construction kits, but you might have to take these apart again to use the kit for something else. Some kits provide parts that you can use only once. The one shown lets you quickly build up boxes and frames for mechanisms.

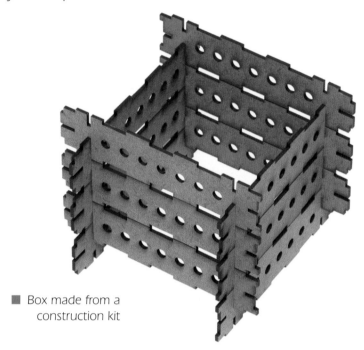

■ Box made from a construction kit

Cardboard

Card is not always very strong, but can be used to try out ideas. This is sometimes called cardboard engineering. A lot of the packaging we throw away will do for making flat mechanisms.

Card is cut with a craft knife, guillotine or scissors. Thin card can be thickened by gluing layers together with stick glue or double-sided tape. This is called laminating. When card is laminated, shaped parts are held together like a sandwich.

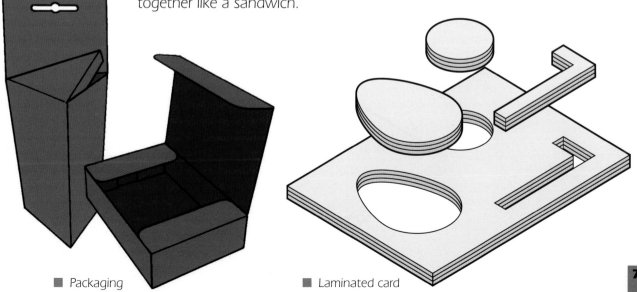

■ Packaging   ■ Laminated card

Holes can be made by piercing with something sharp. The best tool to use is a hole punch. Paper punches will sometimes do, but other special punches are made for card.

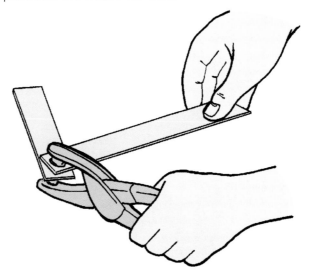

Punched card can be joined with screws and nuts, rivets or paper fasteners. The joints can be either tight, so they do not move, or loose. Care must be taken with the fasteners if the joint is loose.

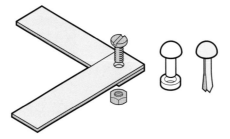

Some mechanisms need parts or joints to be fixed down. This can be done on a soft board or another piece of card if it is stiff enough. Soft board allows you to use drawing or mapping pins for some joints.

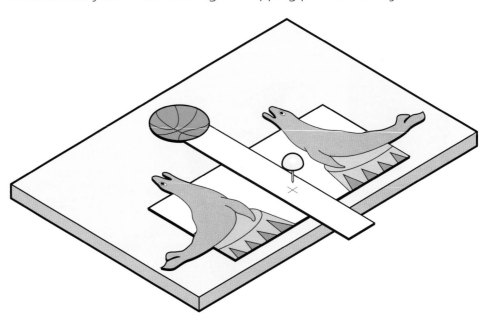

■ Plastic sheet

Thin plastic sheet can be used to make prototypes and real mechanisms. A good material is 1.5 mm polystyrene, which comes in many bright colours. It can be stuck with polystyrene adhesive (used for gluing models) or double-sided tape.

Polystyrene can be shaped using the methods shown on page 40. It is cut with a special guillotine or by scoring and breaking. A line is scored with a ruler and the sheet is then pushed against an edge. It cracks along the score line. It can also be cut with a nibbling tool, which cuts out little pieces of the material.

Thin polystyrene can be drilled but it is easier and safer to use a punch. There are several special punches for this.

Punched polystyrene can be joined in the same way as cardboard.

You can make mechanical parts out of a plastic that softens in hot water. It is called polymorph. If you place the granules in a cup and pour over hot water, it softens so that you can mould it. It goes as hard as normal plastic when it cools down, but you can re-use it by heating again.

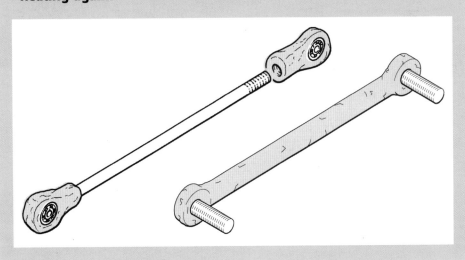

◼ Metal sheet

Metal sheet is often used to make mechanisms (see page 70). Aluminium sheet is ideal because it is light, strong and easy to work with. It comes plain or with a coating. If it is coated you do not have to worry about painting it afterwards. Sheet metal can be fastened with doubled-sided tape.

It is cut either with a special guillotine or a nibbling tool. It can also be cut with shears, but this distorts it. Sheet metal can be folded along a line with a metal folder. This gives you a sharp bend.

Metal can also be put through a special roller, which curves it. If you roll the metal a number of times, you can make a complete cylinder.

The same punches used for plastics are also used for metals.

◼ Metal rods

Aluminium rod can be used to make mechanical parts like cranks and push-rods. It is soft enough to cut with combination pliers and can be bent by hand. If you want to make several parts the same, then a bending jig can be made. This might be a piece of wood with pegs.

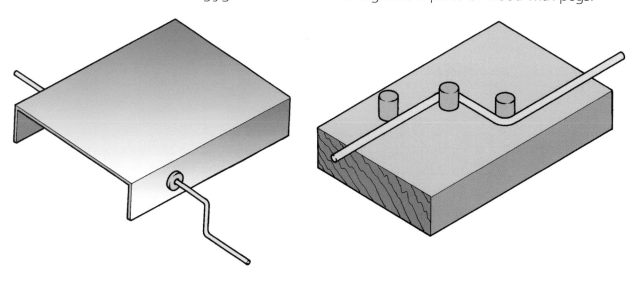

◼ Smartlink

This is a very soft tube that fits tightly over 3 mm diameter rod and makes a flexible joint. It allows one rod to turn another – even around corners. It also allows rods to link up and push backwards and forwards. Because it 'gives' so much, it also allows you to make a few mistakes.

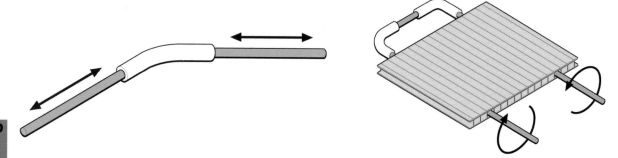

Design and make challenges

Using the 'mechanical words' and 'making mechanisms' guides, you can design many things. When you do the design work, remember that you can use thin card or even paper to try out ideas first.

Balance There are two main families of weighing machines: electronic and mechanical. The mechanical ones are still very popular and are usually low cost. A simple weighing machine consists of just a lever resting on a fulcrum. You place the unknown mass on one side of the lever and masses on the other side until they balance.

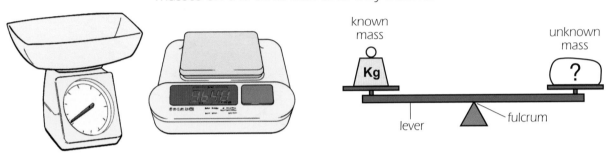

A type of weighing machine called a check-balance tells you if something is under- or overweight. For example, a very accurate check-balance can tell if a small coin is the correct weight. If it uses a simple lever, this has to be able to move very easily but not move too far up and down.

Design and make a check-balance for weighing letters to make sure they are not over the limit for an ordinary first class stamp. Can you make the check-balance disposable?

Magnifyer Magnifying glasses are used in many ways but to work well they need to be held at the correct distance from the things being looked at. Some magnifying glasses have a mechanism that lets you adjust the lens and then leave it in place. Examples of these mechanisms use linkages.

Design and make a magnifying tool for use on a desk. It should use linkages so that it is adjustable for height.

■ Desk magnifying tool

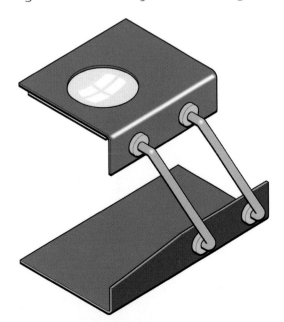

Moving book page
Books sometimes have moving parts. You pull a tab or turn a wheel and something else happens on the page. These pages are usually two pages stuck together around the edge. The mechanism is in the middle. When you design your page, you can forget this and put the mechanism on the back of a sheet of thin card.

Design a page for a book or magazine. Copy the page and then design a moving mechanism so that something happens to make the page more interesting.

Automaton

Models of living things that move like the real thing are called automatons. People have been making them for hundreds of years, and some are very complicated. You can buy books with cut-out card automata or kits of ready-made parts. But it is also very easy to design and make your own.

Design an automaton with at least one moving part. It can be powered by hand or using an electric motor.

A good place to start is with a flat figure with just one or two moving parts. This might be drawn or cut out from a magazine. The figure is glued to card, plastic sheet or even metal to give it stiffness. It is then attached to a base. The picture on the left shows an automaton figure given movement by a cam. This is powered by a gearbox. Other metal rods or wires can be added to give other movements. The automaton shown here on the right is mounted on a base made from clip-together kit parts.

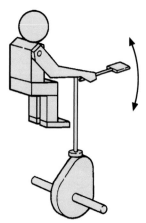

Advertising 'widget'

You may have seen things in shop windows or on counters that move to catch your attention. These range from life-like automata to solar-powered wobblers. Can you design and make an advertising 'widget' to catch peoples' attention in a shop?

The 'widget' you design might be moving all the time or only when it is operated by someone. If it is powered by a motor, it could be stopped and started by an electronic circuit such as IQ (see page 127).

■ This widget is advertising a shoe repair shop

Helping hand

There are many times when people are not able to reach things. You may have seen rubbish being picked up using a spiked stick. Sometimes it is done with something that uses a mechanism to get movement from A to B.

Design and make a helping hand to assist a person to pick up objects that are out of reach. If you cannot make this to full size, then make a moving model to show how it would work.

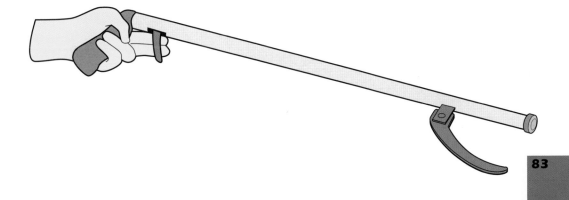

Bug toy In most mechanisms, vibration is not a good thing. It happens when something is spinning and is not balanced – like the drum of a washing machine full of clothes. Sometimes we want to make things vibrate and it is done by spinning a weight or mass off-centre. An example is a dispenser that shakes out powder. Another example is a toy that judders and moves around. Many of these toys have been called bugs because they are made to look like insects.

Design and make a bug that uses a motor with an off-centre mass. This might be a wheel with Blue tac stuck on the edge or a special plastic moulding.

■ This mass is placed off centre on the motor. When the bug head is attached, it will spin and vibrate

Kinetic art machine Many artists use simple mechanisms to create interesting movements. Some of these leave marks behind on a surface. Some of them even make complicated patterns.

Using a mechanism, design and make a kinetic art machine that moves and leaves marks behind on a piece of paper. This can be very simple: for example a two-wheel buggy that drags around a pen. If the wheels are different sizes, it will go around in circles. A more complicated design might use a crank to push a pencil backwards and forwards.

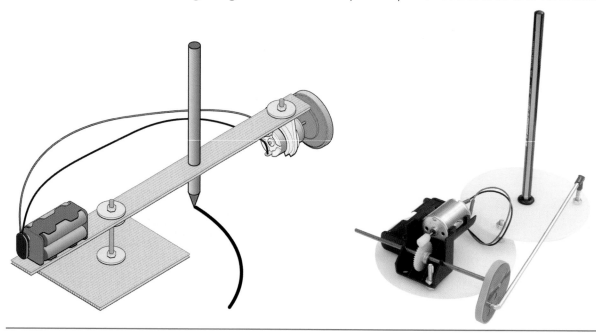

■ Robot challenge

Robots come in many shapes and sizes. They do things that people normally do. Some even look like and move like people. Others have very limited movements and can only repeat these over and over again. All robots use mechanisms of one sort or another. Most working robots tend to be large and complicated, but you can design and make simple robots that move a bit like people or some animals.

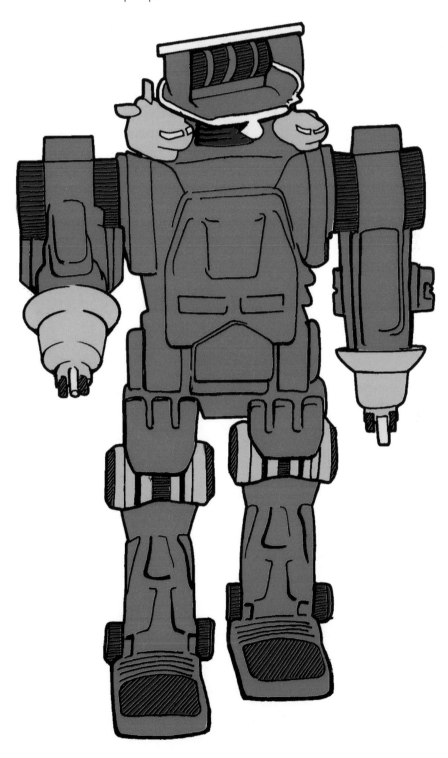

■ Robots with wheels

Many robots move on wheels or tracks. Robots like this are used to move things around or carry cameras to unsafe places.

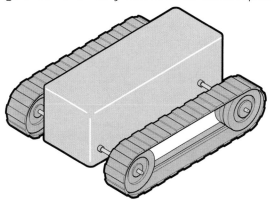

One type uses two motors and gearboxes. It will go backwards or forwards and steer around corners. You need to fix the two power units onto a base (the robot chassis). For example, two clunk–click gearboxes can be fixed to a piece of plastic or metal sheet. Where the back of the plate touches the ground you need a 'skid' so it can be pulled around easily.

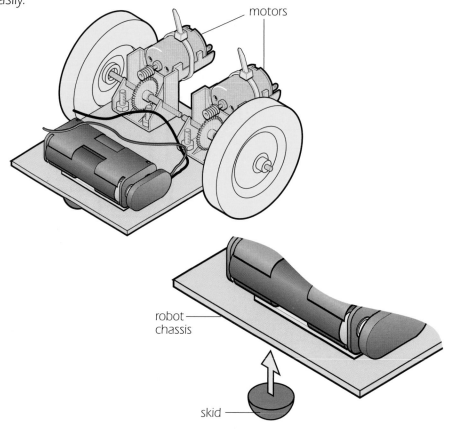

motors

robot chassis

skid

To control this type of robot you need to be able to turn the motors on and off and reverse them. You can make a switch controller with two slide switches (see page 100). The robot can be made to go around an obstacle course. If you want the robot to move by itself, then an IQ board (see page 127) could be added. This can be programmed to turn the motors on or off, but it cannot reverse them.

■ Robots that crawl

Some animals move by crawling along. You can imitate a natural crawling movement with a crank mechanism. If a gearbox unit is fitted with cams, these can pull and push two hooked legs. Going forwards, the hooks will ride over a rough surface like a carpet. But when they go backwards, they dig in and drag the body forwards.

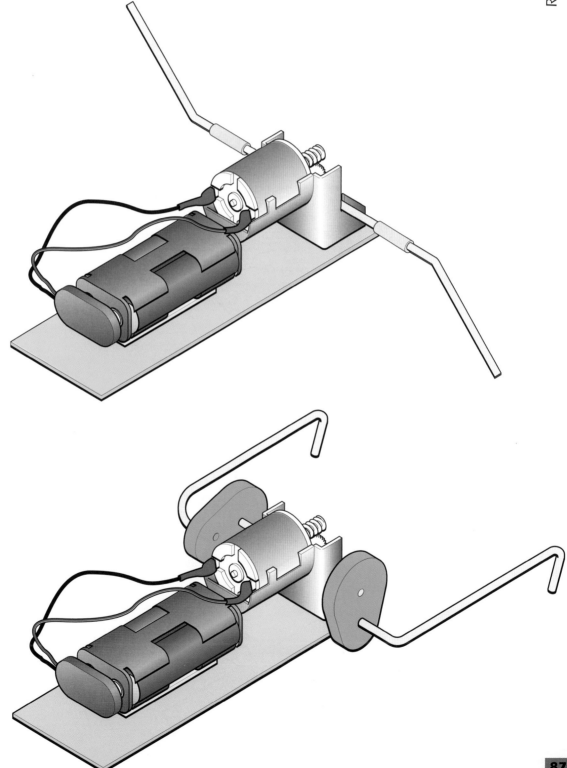

This kind of robot can be fixed to a flexible base to give a pulsing action like a snake. You can use polypropylene sheet and connect it to the rods using smartlink tubing.

Another type of robot has two flipper type legs. When these turn around they will dig into a surface and pull the body along. The movement depends on whether the legs hit the surface together or in turn.

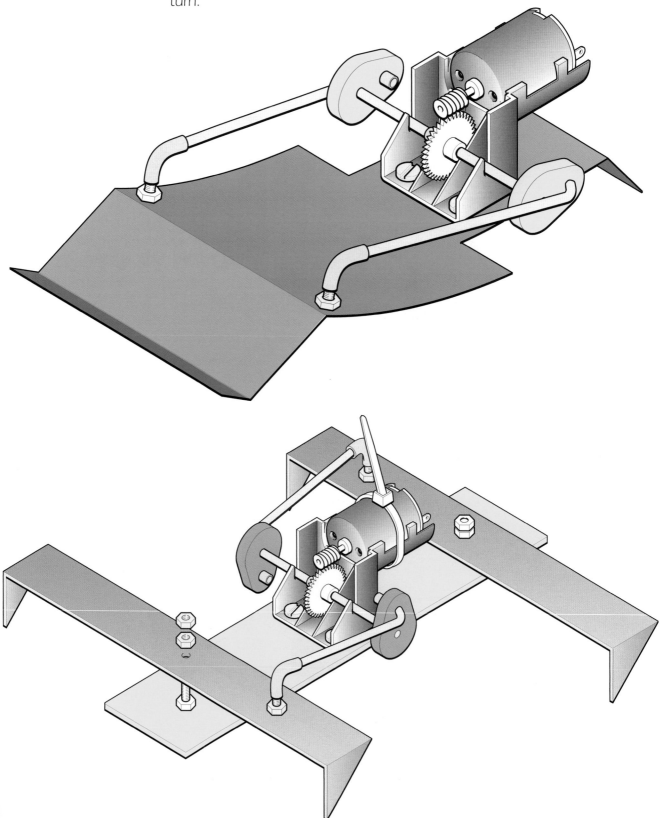

■ Robots that swim

First of all, your robot has to float! The easiest way of getting this to happen is to attach the mechanism to a material like expanded polystyrene. It is then quite easy to think of ways of making flippers that dip in and out of water. For example, if the ends of a gearbox shaft are slightly bent, they will give a pair of flippers a paddling movement. The flippers can easily be made from Correx – a plastic version of corrugated cardboard.

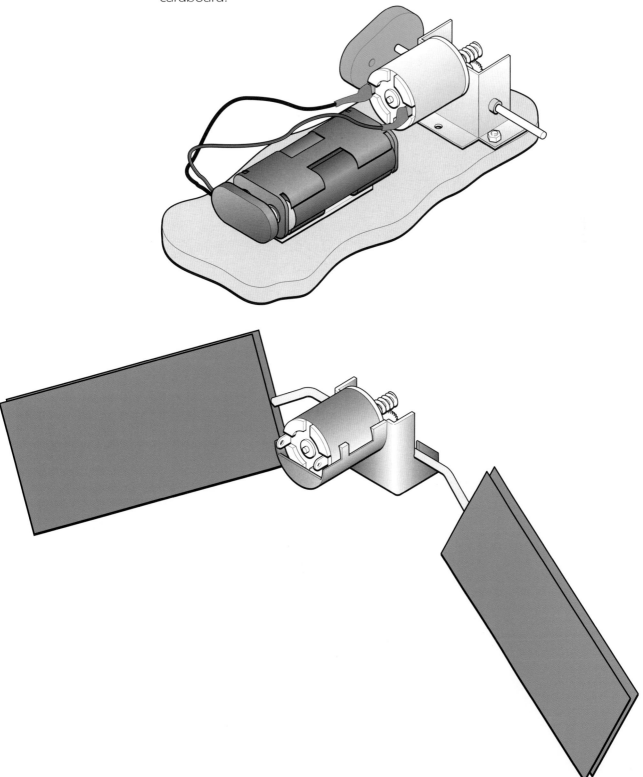

A more complicated swimmer uses cams to push and pull a pair of folded flippers. When these are pushed backwards, they open out in the water and the robot moves forwards. When they are pulled back, they close up and slip through the water more easily. The flippers can be made from polypropylene which is tough and flexible.

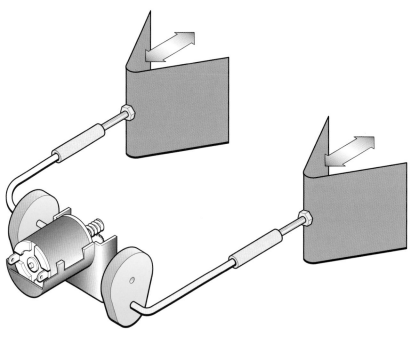

Robot swimmers can also imitate fish and use a tail movement just like the real thing. If you can fasten the end of a length of flexible plastic sheet, you can make it ripple like a fin. This is done by connecting it to a rod from a cam with smartlink tubing. When the sheet is moved backwards and forwards, it causes a rippling movement.

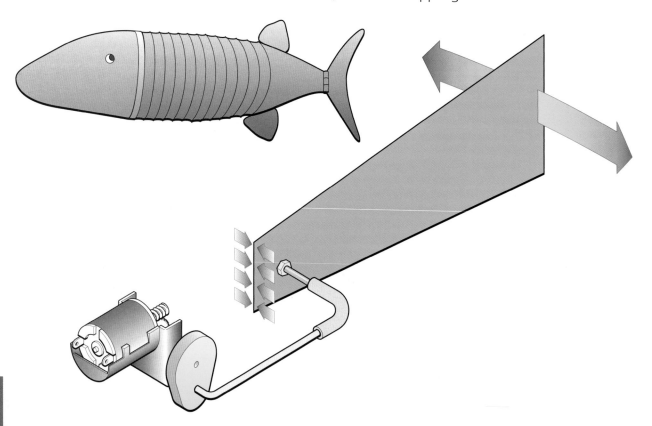

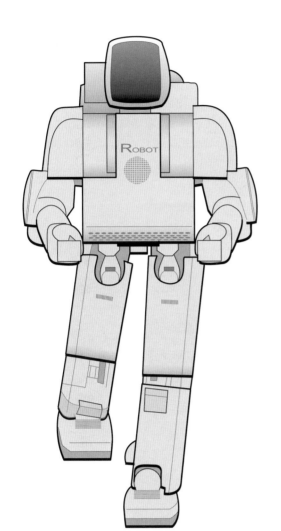

■ Robots that walk

Robots that walk like people are probably the most difficult to design and make. A robot that really walks like a human has only just been made after millions of pounds were spent on its development!

One of the biggest problems of a robot with two legs is keeping balance. You can solve this problem with a balancing trick that some dinosaurs used – a long tail – but how many humans have you seen with a tail?

A simple walking movement is produced when two cams are connected to legs. When the cams turn, they give the legs an up and down movement. If the legs pass through holes, they also move backwards and forwards. But remember: it is very important in this type of robot that everything lines up and moves freely or it will not keep balance.

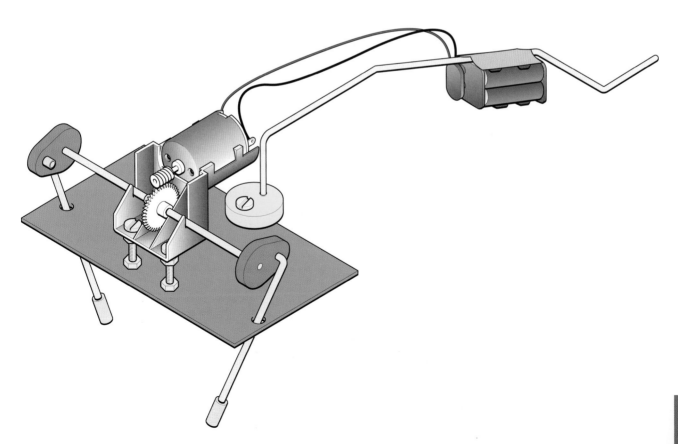

Small mechanical miracles

Modern products tend to have fewer mechanisms and mechanical parts than they used to. Computers and printers, for example, have very few mechanical parts. But if you go back only 30 years, people were still using mechanical typewriters to produce typed text. These had hundreds of moving parts.

Electronics has taken over many of the things that were previously mechanical. However, we will always need mechanisms for certain tasks. A colourful example is the electrical stapling machine shown here.

In the future, many of the mechanisms we use will be too small to see. This is because they are being made by the same techniques used for making electronic chips. Scientists are now able to make electric motors that will fit onto the head of a pin – and they are already getting smaller!

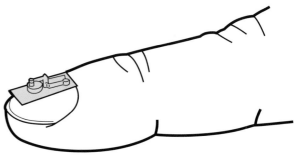

6 Electronics in control

You press a button, and something happens. By pressing a button on a torch, you control the light. If you press a button on a washing machine, something far more complicated happens. The washing machine takes over and controls the washing and drying. When you press buttons on a mobile phone, you might well be sending signals around the world via satellites in space. These things all depend on electronic circuits.

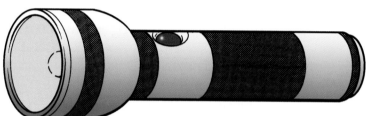

A circuit consists of two or more parts (called components) connected together. A simple torch has a switch and a bulb. Your mobile phone may contain millions of microscopic components. There are many circuits that you can design and make using only a few modern components. You just need to understand what these components do and a few basic rules.

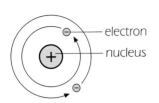

■ Structure of an atom

Electrons in electronics

All matter consists of atoms, and these are made up of even smaller parts. One of these parts is called an electron. When a number of electrons move through a material, we talk about an electric current flowing. Some of the words people use to talk about electricity are the same words used to describe water.

Q Try to recognise these water words as you work through this unit.

Current flows easily in metals such as copper and aluminium. These are good conductors. It hardly flows at all in materials such as plastics. These are insulators.

Electrical conductors	Electrical insulators
copper	wood
aluminium	plastics
steel	paper
iron	cotton
brass	rubber
silver	glass
gold	leather

This is why electrical wires and cables have a metal core surrounded by a protecting plastic sleeve.

Electricity supplies

A battery is one source of electric current. It is a kind of electric pump. When a conductor is connected between the terminals on a battery, chemical changes inside make electrons move from the negative (–) to the positive (+) side. It was believed many years ago that electric current was a kind of fluid that flowed from + to –, so we still talk about electric current as if it flows from + to –. This is called conventional current flow.

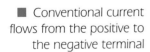
tip
* You have to be careful with batteries. If you connect a wire between the two terminals, a very large current will flow. The battery gets hot and it quickly goes 'flat'.

■ Conventional current flows from the positive to the negative terminal

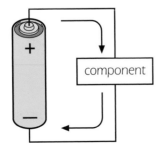

component

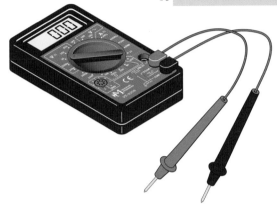

■ Measuring electricity

We measure electricity and the way it flows in a circuit with a multimeter. A digital multimeter shows the measurements as numbers on a display. It will measure three things:

1 Voltage If you think of a battery as a pump, the voltage is a measure of pressure. This is measured in volts.

■ Measuring the voltage of a battery

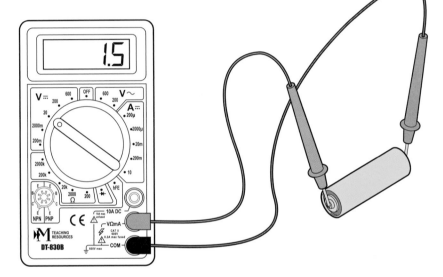

2 Current This is the quantity of electricity flowing. It is measured in amps. For most electronics work we use a smaller unit called a milliamp (mA). 1 mA is $\frac{1}{1000}$ of an amp.

■ Measuring the current flow through a motor

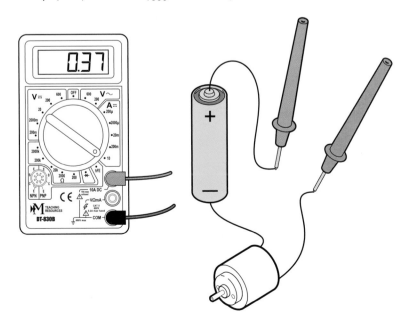

3 Resistance Resistance limits the flow of current. It is measured in ohms. A short length of copper (a good conductor) has almost no resistance. Paper (a good insulator) has very high resistance. Materials such as a graphite (in a pencil lead) have a resistance somewhere in between.

■ Measuring the resistance of a material

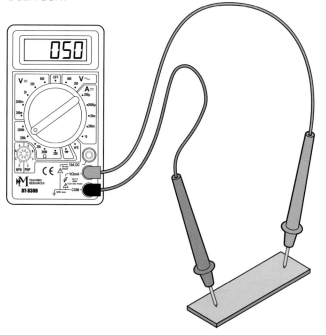

Digital multimeters are now as cheap as calculators and are very easy to use.

exercise

1 Try measuring the resistance of different materials, including a line drawn on paper with a soft pencil.

If you set the multimeter to the high resistance range, you can measure your own resistance. In fact the reading you get depends on how moist your skin is. Lie detectors make use of changes in skin moisture, because it increases if you are telling a lie. So, the multimeter might become a lie detector.

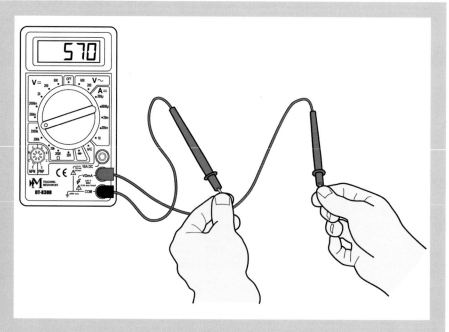

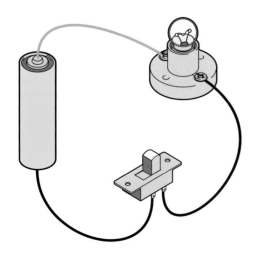

■ Circuits

A torch has a very simple circuit. It consists of a battery, bulb and switch connected in a loop. When the switch is 'off', it breaks the circuit loop and no electricity flows. When the switch is 'on', electric current flows around the loop from one terminal of the battery to the other, and the bulb lights up.

■ Drawing circuits

It would become very confusing if we drew circuits as they look. Instead, we use straight lines and special pictures (symbols) to stand for the components. These are called circuit diagrams.

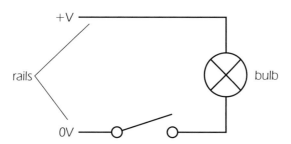

A circuit diagram for the torch has straight lines drawn at 90° to each other, but it is still a loop. Normally, we don't even bother to show where the electricity comes from. The diagram has a top and bottom line called rails. The top is marked +V and the bottom marked –V (and sometimes 0 V).

■ Series and parallel connections

Connecting components in series means joining them in a row, like sausages. An example is the bulbs in Christmas tree lights.

Connecting components in parallel means joining them side by side. An example is two bulbs in a torch to give more light.

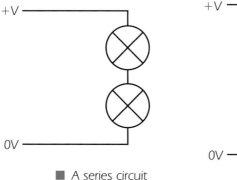

■ A series circuit

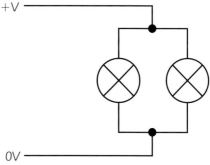

■ A parallel circuit

■ Making circuits

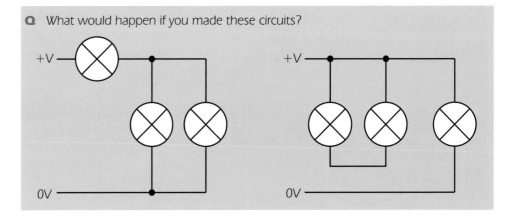

Q What would happen if you made these circuits?

So, how would you make the torch circuit? There are many different ways of connecting components. For trying things out, we use temporary connections:

Example 1: Screw terminal blocks   Screw terminal blocks are made for electricians who want to connect electrical cables together. They do very well for connecting wires to components.

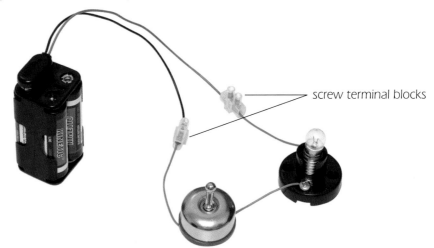

screw terminal blocks

Example 2: Pin block   A pin block is a polythene block with small holes. If you put two wires into a hole, they can be locked in place by pushing in a small pin.

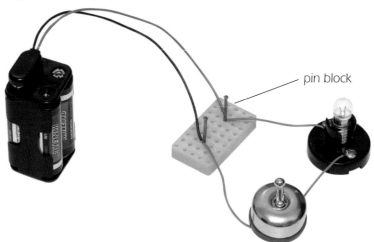

pin block

Example 3: Spring board   A spring board has rows of small springs. When a spring is bent over, wires can be wedged into the side, and the spring holds them together.

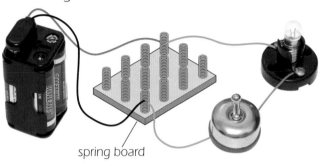

spring board

Example 4: Prototyping board   A prototyping board is a special board with rows of small holes connected underneath. If you put wires in holes in the same row, they will connect together.

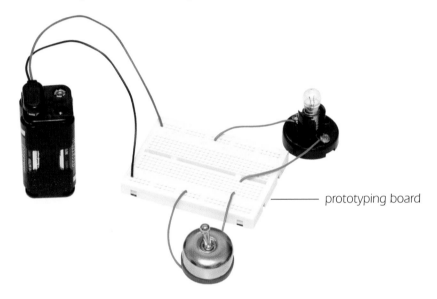

prototyping board

■ A permanent circuit board

Circuits in products such as telephones are permanent circuits, called printed circuits. These consist of thin lines of copper on a board. Wires and components are connected by soldered joints. The solder is a mixture of metals that melts at a low temperature and makes a permanent joint. The lines of copper (called tracks) can be on the same side of the board as the components – or on the other side with wires and legs passing through holes. (See page 129 for making printed circuit boards.)

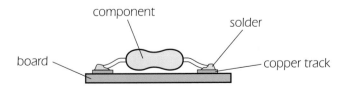

component

solder

board

copper track

■ Copper tracks on the same side as the components

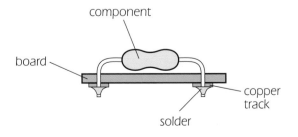

component

board

copper track

solder

■ Copper tracks on the opposite side to the components

■ Switches

These come in many shapes and sizes, but they all have the same job to do. They let electric current flow or they stop it flowing.

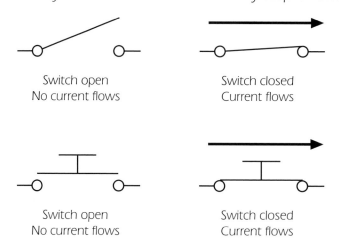

Switch open
No current flows

Switch closed
Current flows

Switch open
No current flows

Switch closed
Current flows

Press button switches

The type of switch you use on a computer keyboard or phone is called a press-to-make switch. It connects or completes a circuit when you press it and then springs back.

■ Press-to-make switch

Latching type switches

The type of switch you use on cycle lights and house lighting clicks from one position to another and stays either on or off. There are many types: slide switch, toggle switch and rocker switch. These often have more than two connections on the outside because each is designed to switch more than one thing.

■ Slide switch   ■ Toggle switch   ■ Rocker switch

Membrane panel switches

These are the 'touch' switches found on many vending machines and some calculators. They are a form of press to make switch. They are made using layers of thin plastic. Membrane switches can be made using paper and aluminium foil or tape.

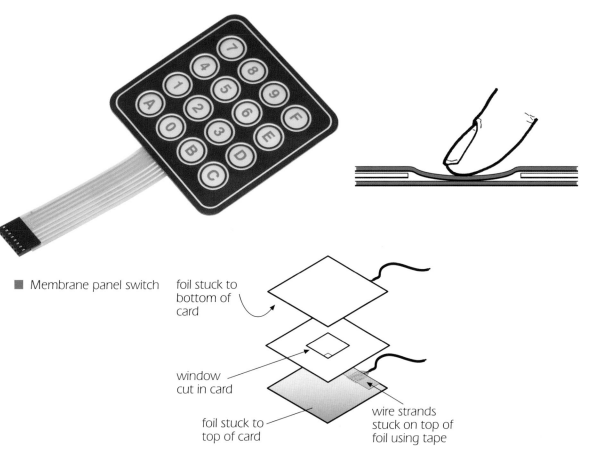

■ Membrane panel switch

foil stuck to bottom of card

window cut in card

foil stuck to top of card

wire strands stuck on top of foil using tape

Special switches

There are many other types of switch.

A reed switch turns on when you place a magnet nearby. These are used in burglar alarm systems.

A float switch in a tank turns on when the level of water rises.

Very often, it is possible to make special switches out of scrap components.

■ Reed switch

■ Float switch

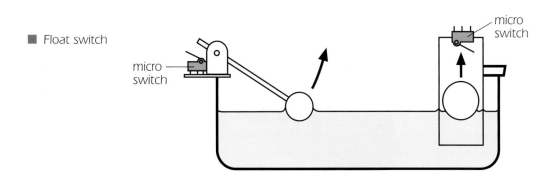

micro switch

micro switch

When you turn a switch off, a small electrical spark can jump across the contacts. This causes radio interference. A few years ago someone discovered that the ignition spark from a cigarette lighter could open electric car park barriers.

■ Circuits with a switch

A small lamp

A bulb contains a metal filament that heats up and glows white. Some bulbs have special filaments and gas inside that makes them very bright. The bulb will be marked with a voltage, and the battery should be chosen to match this. A torch or light circuit can be made using the terminal block connection method (see page 98).

The largest bulb you can buy is one million times larger than the smallest.

A door buzzer

■ Buzzer

■ Buzzer circuit symbol

There are many components that make a sound when current flows through them. Some of these contain a small circuit to make the sound and must be connected in the circuit the correct way round, for example, red wire to +. Normally the switch in a buzzer circuit is on a long lead and the battery and buzzer are together. Instead of buying a press switch, you can make a membrane panel (see page 101).

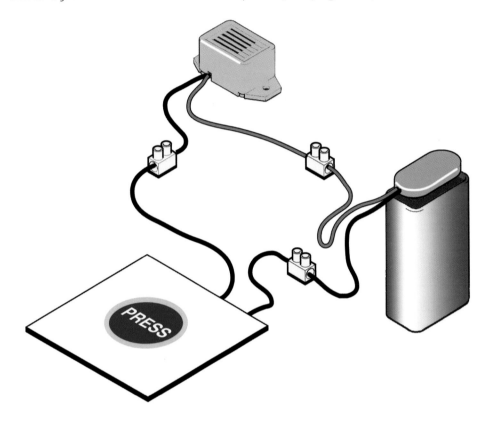

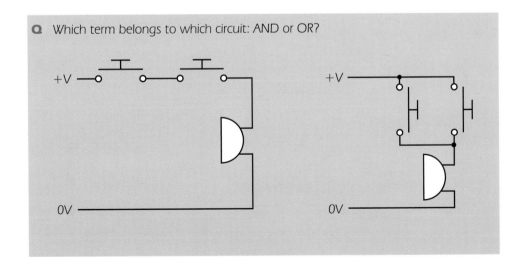

Q Which term belongs to which circuit: AND or OR?

Early electric door bells used miniature church bells to make the sound.

■ Light-emitting diodes (LEDs)

A diode is a circuit component which only lets current flow in one direction. An LED is a special type of diode. LEDs are replacing bulbs for lighting. They use less electricity than bulbs, last longer and do not get hot. Most bright LEDs are suitable for torches, but those giving out white light can be more expensive. LEDs need to be connected to a battery the correct way round, otherwise they don't work. The leg next to a small flat side on the case should be connected to –.

LEDs can be connected either in parallel or in series. In series, they get dimmer.

■ LEDs

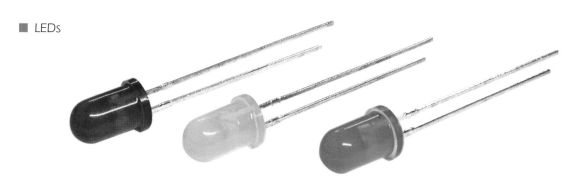

■ LED circuit symbol

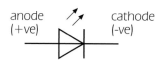

anode (+ve)   cathode (-ve)

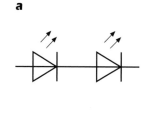

flat side

anode (+ve)

cathode (-ve)

tip
* Warning: Most LEDs need to be connected in a circuit with a resistor (see page 107). This prevents too much current flowing and damaging the LED.

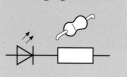

a

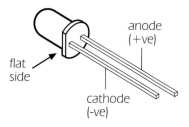

■ LEDs connected in series

b

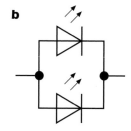

■ LEDs connected in parallel

Q Why do LEDs get dimmer when they are in series?

■ Circuits with LEDs

If you use a thin, round lithium battery, you can design and make a tiny torch without a normal switch (or a resistor). The legs of the LED do not normally touch the two sides of battery, but when the torch is squeezed, the LED connects and lights up.

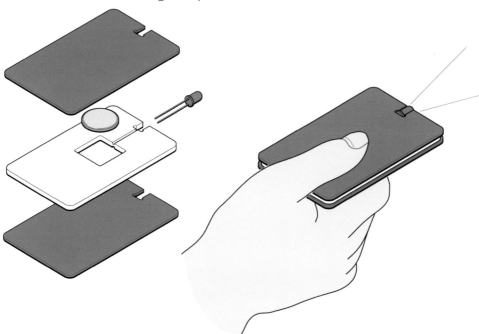

Warning light

Flashing LEDs have a built-in circuit that turns on and off. These can be used to create warning lamps to warn people of danger at night, for example, around scaffolding.

Moisture detector

A small amount of current will flow through wet or moist earth (but not if it is dry). This is the basis for a moisture detector for plants, etc. A circuit is made (using a 9 V battery) and instead of a switch, there are two metal rods (probes). When the probes are put into damp earth, the LED lights up. (Note the resistor in the circuit.)

■ Moisture sensor

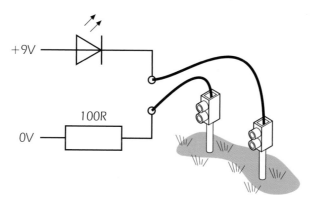

Fizzy drinks are better conductors than flat ones. Try measurements with a multimeter or your moisture detector circuit.

Signalling

Old telegraph communication systems used just a single wire and the ground to complete a circuit loop. Earth is actually an excellent conductor of electricity. The circuit shown would enable you to signal over long distances, but the earth must be wet around the rods.

■ Single wire telegraph

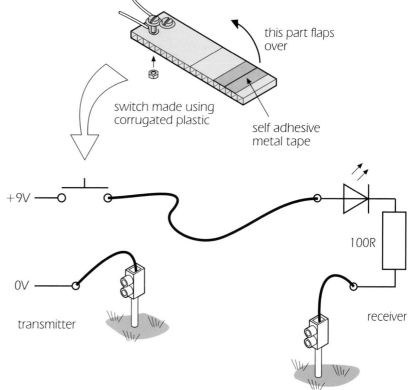

You can use the earth as an extension lead for your radio. Plug it in as shown, making sure that the earth pins are wide apart.

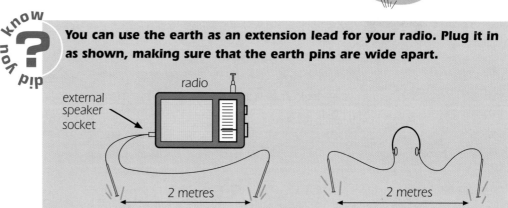

Q What would happen if you made the following circuits?

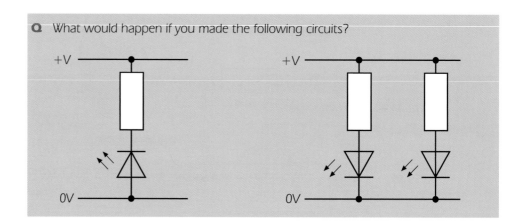

Resistors

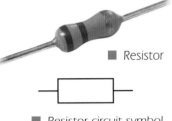
■ Resistor

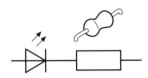
■ Resistor circuit symbol

A resistor limits the flow of current in a circuit. Resistance is measured in ohms (Ω). A 1 R (1 ohm) resistor offers almost no resistance, a 1 k (1 kilo ohm) resistor offers medium resistance and a 1 M (1 million ohm) resistor is almost an insulator. There are many resistance values in between. The most common resistors are made of carbon and have different coloured stripes for different values. The diagram explains how to read a resistor value.

When resistors are connected in series, the values are added up. Two 1 k resistors in series give a value of 2 k.

When resistors are connected in parallel, the total resistance reduces. Two 1 k resistors connected in parallel give a value of 500 ohms.

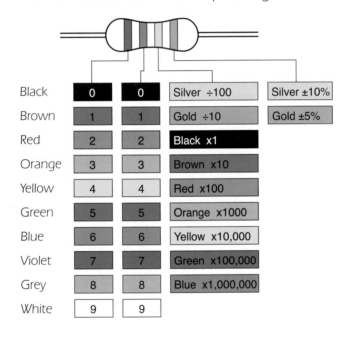

Black	0	0	Silver ÷100	Silver ±10%
Brown	1	1	Gold ÷10	Gold ±5%
Red	2	2	Black x1	
Orange	3	3	Brown x10	
Yellow	4	4	Red x100	
Green	5	5	Orange x1000	
Blue	6	6	Yellow x10,000	
Violet	7	7	Green x100,000	
Grey	8	8	Blue x1,000,000	
White	9	9		

Example shown = 560 KΩ ± 5%

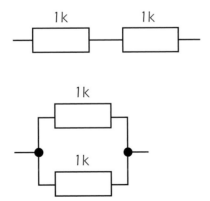

You can make a high value resistor by drawing a heavy line on paper with a very soft pencil. The pencil's graphite (a form of carbon) is a good resistor if the pencil is rubbed several times over the line.

■ Variable resistors

Variable resistors alter in value when you turn or slide something. These are used, for example, as volume controls.

■ Variable resistor

■ Variable resistor circuit symbol

■ Special resistors

Light-dependent resistor (LDR)

A light-dependent resistor (LDR) changes its value when light falls on it. An LDR has a high resistance in the dark (for example, 100 k) and a low resistance in bright light (for example, 100 ohms). LDRs allow circuits to respond to different light levels.

■ Light-dependent resistor

■ Light-dependent resistor symbol

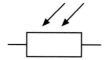

Thermistor

A thermistor changes its value when it warms up. One type of thermistor has a high resistance when cold (for example, 47 k) and a low resistance when hot (for example, 1 k). Thermistors allow circuits to respond to different temperatures.

■ Thermistor

■ Thermistor circuit symbol

■ Circuits with resistors

LED torch

A resistor is used with ordinary LEDs to limit current and prevent damage – as in an LED torch or lamp. As a rough rule, resistance of 50 ohms per volt is used to be safe. For example, if you have a 3 V battery, use a 150 ohm resistor or as close as you can get to this.

■ LED torch circuit

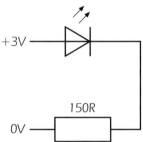

+3V

150R

0V

On a dark night the pilot of an aircraft can pick out a single ultra-bright LED from the ground if you point it skywards.

Fuse tester

A simple LED circuit can be used to test fuses. If a gap is left in the circuit loop, nothing happens. If this is bridged with a good fuse, current will flow through it and the LED will light up. If the fuse is blown, nothing happens.

■ Fuse tester circuit

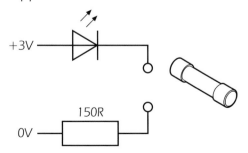

+3V

150R

0V

A few years ago LEDs cost £s each. Today they cost just pence.

Resistor dimmers

A variable resistor can be used to dim an LED. Normally, a fixed resistor is also used for safety. This prevents the resistance in the circuit falling to zero, which might damage the LED, if the variable resistor is set to zero.

■ A dimmer circuit

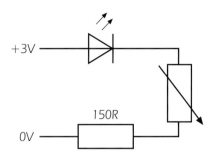

Many different materials conduct electricity, some better than others. So, many things can be turned into variable resistors in an emergency. These include pencils, pots of water and even fruit!

Battery tester

Resistors heat up when current flows through them. Sometimes special wire is used as a resistor when we want this to happen. If you want to test whether a battery is flat or not, you can connect it to a length of resistance wire. If the battery can warm the wire up, then it is not flat. To detect the warmth of the wire, we can use a small piece of heat-sensitive film. The film changes colour when heated.

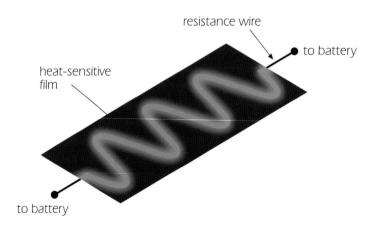

resistance wire

to battery

heat-sensitive film

to battery

Special edition CD cases have been printed with heat-sensitive ink. They change colour when you touch them.

Light meter

An LDR and multimeter can be used as a light meter. The more light, the lower the meter voltage reading.

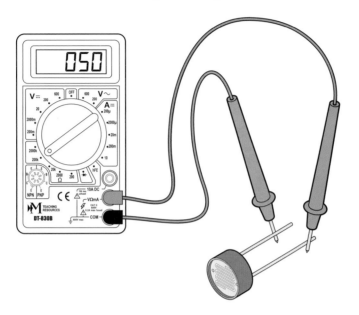

Thermometer

A thermistor and multimeter can be used as a thermometer. The higher the temperature, the lower the meter voltage reading.

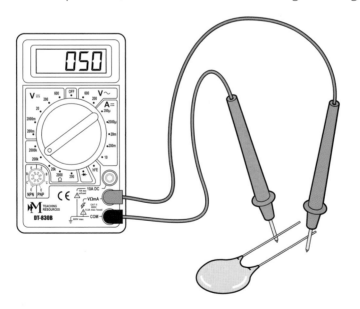

Modern 'smart' glass can change colour to filter out light and heat. Some sunglasses and spectacles work in this way.

Q   If you were stranded somewhere and needed to make a variable resistor in an emergency, how would you do this with only some apples and nails?

Capacitors

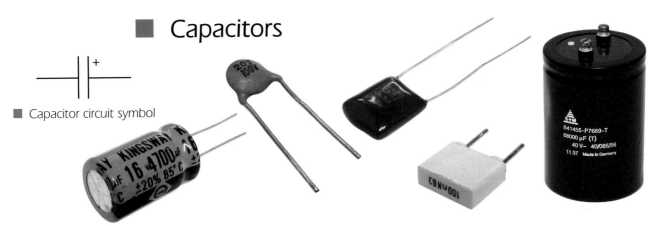

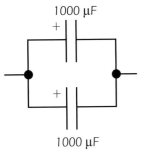

■ Capacitor circuit symbol

1000 μF
+

+

1000 μF
■ Capacitors in parallel

A capacitor stores electricity. If you connect a capacitor to a battery, it charges up very quickly. It then discharges if you connect it to something like an LED. Although capacitors differ in actual size, their storage size is measured in units called farads (F). Because even 1 F is very large, capacitors used in electronics are measured in much smaller units – microfarads (μF). 1 μF is one millionth of a farad. A 2200 μF capacitor will light up an LED for several seconds before it goes 'flat' and needs recharging.

If you connect capacitors in parallel, the values add up. Two 1000 μF capacitors connected in parallel have a value of 2000 μF.

Super capacitor

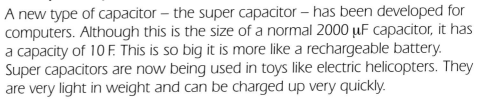

A new type of capacitor – the super capacitor – has been developed for computers. Although this is the size of a normal 2000 μF capacitor, it has a capacity of 10 F. This is so big it is more like a rechargeable battery. Super capacitors are now being used in toys like electric helicopters. They are very light in weight and can be charged up very quickly.

Circuits with capacitors

Auto turn-off

Many appliances turn off automatically after a given time to save battery life. A very simple turn-off circuit can be made with a capacitor, resistor and LED. When the switch is pressed briefly, the LED lights up **and** the capacitor charges up almost instantly. When you take your finger off the switch, the capacitor now supplies current to the LED and keeps it on for a few seconds. The time the LED stays on depends on the value of the resistor and the size of the capacitor. The larger the capacitor and the higher the resistor value, the longer the LED stays on, as shown in the graph below. This circuit might be useful for a small LED torch.

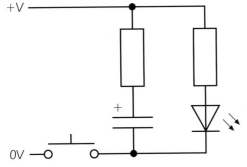

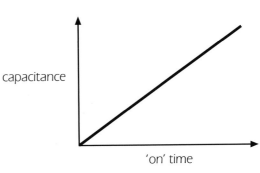

capacitance

'on' time

■ Auto turn-off circuit

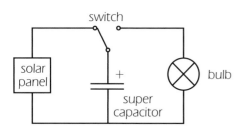

Solar-powered torch

A super capacitor can be charged up from a small solar panel. The circuit shown is for a simple solar-powered torch.

■ Solar-powered torch circuit

Wiggly wire game

Wiggly wire games are sold in many shops, but they are very easy to make. In place of a switch to turn a light or buzzer on, the game has a wire loop that passes over a length of wire. When these two touch, a buzzer sounds or the LED comes on. The problem is that the loop and wire might touch so quickly that you don't see the LED light up. If a capacitor is added, the LED will stay on a little longer and let you know contact was made. This works in the same way as the auto turn-off circuit.

■ Wiggly wire circuit

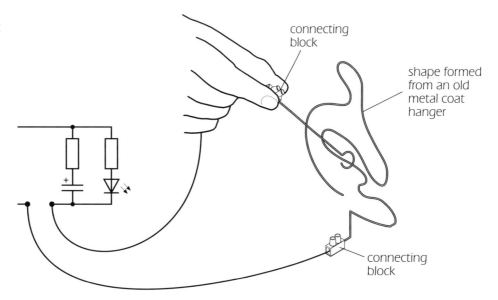

connecting block

shape formed from an old metal coat hanger

connecting block

Electronic money box

If you want a light to come on when a coin is dropped into a box, a capacitor circuit can be used. The circuit needs a micro-switch. This is turned on by a small force or light weight such as a coin.

You can make a micro-switch of your own using pieces of very thin metal.

■ Micro-switch

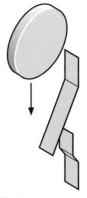

■ Home-made micro-switch

Although they knew very little about electricity, the ancient Greeks and Romans did have coin-in-the-slot machines.

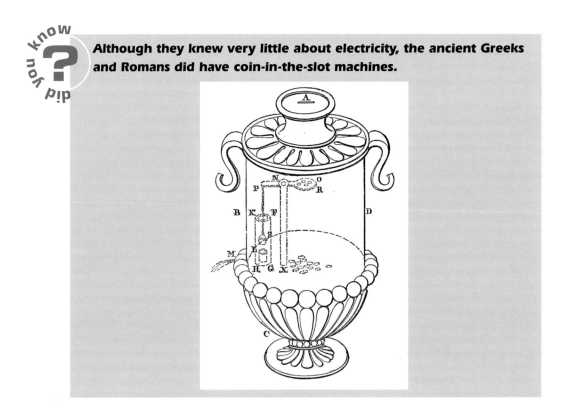

Transistors

A transistor is a component that controls current flow. A common transistor (BC108) has three legs, called collector (C), emitter (E) and base (B). If C and E are connected in a simple circuit, the transistor acts as a switch turned off. If a small current flows to the base, it causes a much larger current to flow between C and E. This is like a switch turned on.

■ Transistors

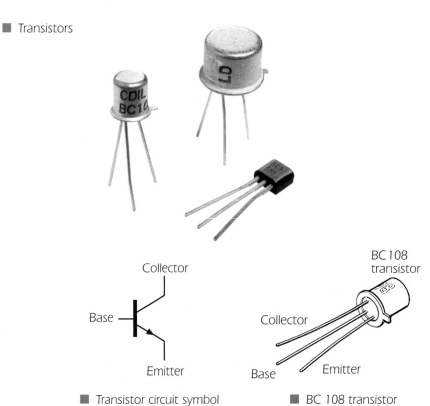

Collector

Base

Emitter

BC 108
transistor

Collector

Base   Emitter

■ Transistor circuit symbol   ■ BC 108 transistor

But why not just use an ordinary switch in a circuit to turn things on and off? The answer is that we often want small currents to control big ones. The example circuit shows a very simple touch switch. Normally, not enough current will pass if you simply complete a circuit with your finger. The resistance across the skin is too high. (Try measuring it with a meter.) However, the small current that does pass is enough to make the transistor turn on to light up the LED.

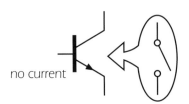
no current

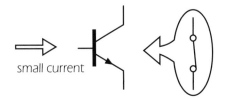
small current

■ With no current flowing into the base, the transistor is switched off

■ With a small current flowing into the base, the transistor is switched on

■ Touch switch circuit

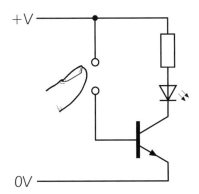

Before transistors, circuits used valves.

If you tried to make a mobile phone with valves, you would need a space the size of St Paul's Cathedral!

■ Circuits with transistors

Moisture detector with buzzer

This circuit can be used to detect moisture or water. It turns on a buzzer when moisture or water passes a small current to the transistor base. This is not possible unless a transistor is used.

■ In damp conditions a small current flows into the base of the transistor so the buzzer is on

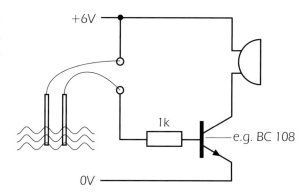

Transistor timer

In this circuit, the transistor acts as a switch. It is normally 'off' so the LED does not light up. When the switch is pressed, the capacitor charges up very quickly. When you take your finger off the switch, the capacitor provides current to the base of the transistor. This keeps it turned on until the capacitor has discharged. The length of time the LED stays on depends on the size of the capacitor.

■ When the touch switch is pressed a current flows through the transistor and the LED stays on for some time after the switch is released

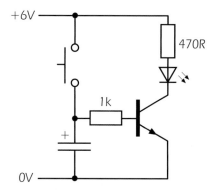

Transistor alarm

Circuits with a switch   This circuit is the same as the timer circuit but a buzzer is swapped for the LED. This means that after a switch is pressed, the buzzer stays running for long enough to warn someone. This happens even though the switch might be operated for less than a second.

■ When the touch switch is pressed a current flows through the transistor and the buzzer stays on for some time after the switch is released

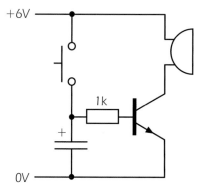

■ Mat switch

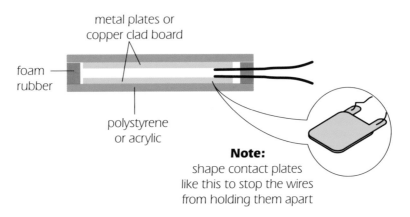

metal plates or
copper clad board

foam
rubber

polystyrene
or acrylic

Note:
shape contact plates
like this to stop the wires
from holding them apart

You can design and make all sorts of switches to trigger this alarm.
One type is a membrane panel switch called a mat switch. Another type
is a tilt switch (see page 122).

Circuits with a light-dependent resistor   In the dark an LDR has a
very high resistance and does not pass much current. In the light the
resistance falls and it passes more current. If you connect an LDR
between the +V and the transistor base, the LDR turns on the transistor
when it is light. If the LDR is placed in the dark under a valuable object,
the alarm sounds if the object is lifted up to allow light to the LDR.

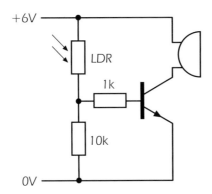

■ Transistor games

Transistors can be used to make games. For example, you can draw lines
on paper with a very soft pencil and use these as part of a circuit. A
treasure hunt game might have a grid of graphite lines hidden under a
cover sheet. You have to find the right spot by using a probe to make
contact with the line. When you find the spot, the LDR will light up.

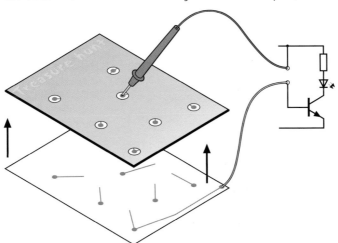

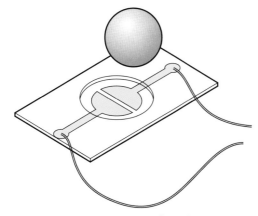

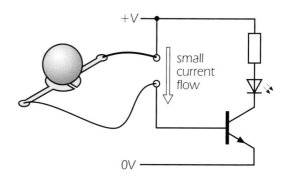

small current flow

■ A ball switch is used in some games

Another example is the type of game where a steel ball has to be rolled into a hole. If there are two contacts in the hole, the ball falling in acts as a kind of switch. Usually, though, the ball will not make very good contact and only pass a small current. This might not be enough for an LED or buzzer connected directly, but it will probably be enough to turn on the transistor.

know ? did you

Many switch contacts are plated with pure gold so that they conduct better.

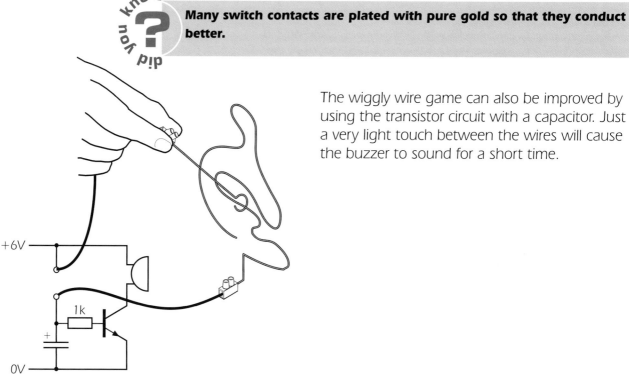

The wiggly wire game can also be improved by using the transistor circuit with a capacitor. Just a very light touch between the wires will cause the buzzer to sound for a short time.

■ Improved wiggly wire circuit

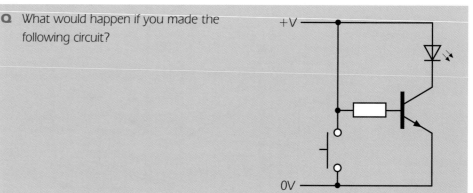

Q What would happen if you made the following circuit?

Field effect transistors (FETs)

Like the transistors already discussed, FETs have three legs, but the legs have different names. They are much more sensitive than the other type and can switch on a very large current. For example, using a high power FET you can switch on a large electric motor just by connecting the gate to +V with a graphite pencil line.

■ FET

■ FET circuit symbol

(D)

(G)

(S)

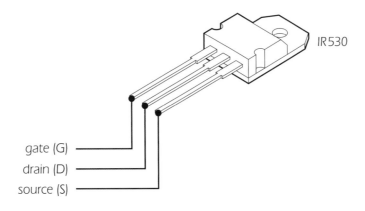

IR530

gate (G)

drain (D)

source (S)

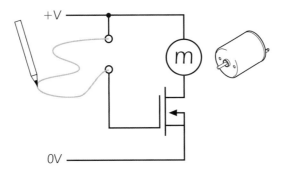

+V

m

0V

■ Circuits with FETs

An FET can do everything that the other transistor circuits can do. You can substitute the other transistor for the FET. Some FETs are 'smart' because they have a tiny circuit built in that protects them against overheating or the wrong voltage.

■ FET used in light-sensing circuit

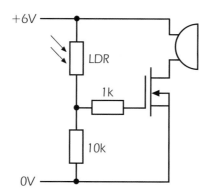

If you leave the gate of an FET unconnected, it doesn't matter whether it is switched on or off. It is so sensitive that you can influence it from a few centimetres away using static. A balloon rubbed on a jumper will affect it, or, if your clothes have a static charge, just waving your hand will do.

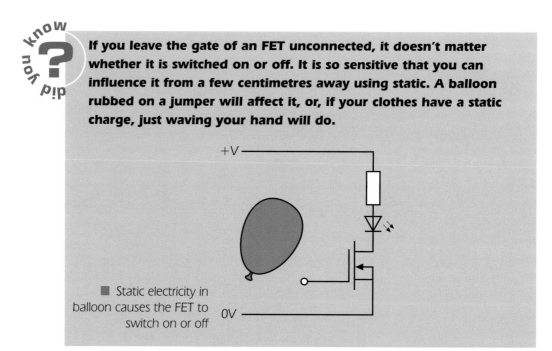

■ Static electricity in balloon causes the FET to switch on or off

Q What would happen if you made the following circuit?

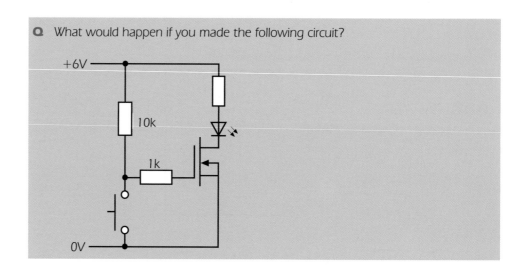

Thyristors

A thyristor has three legs like a transistor but, again, the legs have different names. It can also be connected in the same sort of circuit. Unlike a transistor though, when it switches on, it stays on. By connecting the gate to +V for a fraction of a second, the thyristor turns on. This is called 'triggering' the thyristor. The thyristor turns off again when the battery is disconnected. If the circuit has an on/off switch, then the thyristor can be reset by very quickly turning the switch off and then on again.

■ Thyristor

■ Thyristor circuit symbol

(A)
(G)
(C)

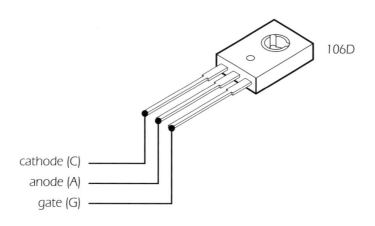

106D

cathode (C)
anode (A)
gate (G)

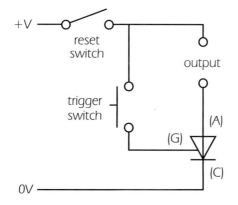

+V
reset switch
trigger switch
output
(A)
(G)
(C)
0V

■ Circuits with thyristors

Thyristor alarms

Circuits with switches   A switch connected between +V and the thyristor gate will act as a trigger to turn on the thyristor and keep a buzzer running. The alarm can only be turned off by disconnecting the battery. A switch to do this can be hidden.

You can make different types of trigger switch to connect to the thyristor. These include membrane switches (see page 101), tilt switches and trembler switches.

■ A trigger switch circuit

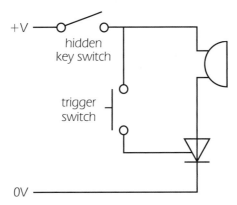

■ A tilt switch – the thyristor is triggered when the switch is tilted

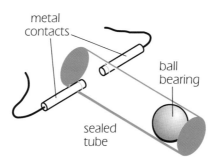

■ A trembler switch – the thyristor is triggered when the switch is suddenly moved

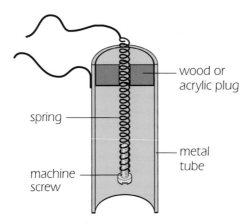

There are old patents for alarms that used exploding gunpowder to warn thieves way.

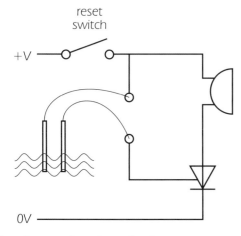

reset
switch

+V

0V

■ A water warning alarm circuit

Circuits with sensors The thyristor can also be switched on by quite small currents passing to the gate. Because water conducts, you can use two wire probes as a switch. We call this a sensor rather than a switch because it responds to a change, wet instead of dry. This alarm might be used to warn that a bath has filled up or when water has risen too high.

LDRs or thermistors can be used as sensors for light and temperature. The LDR or thermistor is connected to the thyristor gate. When light falls on the LDR or the thermistor warms up, the thyristor is triggered. You can adjust the sensitivity of these circuits by adding a variable resistor. The lower the value of the resistor, the less sensitive the circuit.

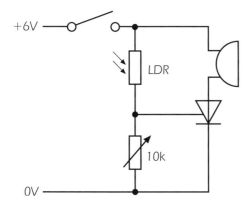

+6V

LDR

10k

0V

■ The buzzer sounds when the light level increases

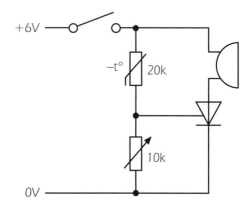

+6V

−t° 20k

10k

0V

■ The buzzer sounds when the temperature increases

know? did you

The first medical instruments for measuring heart beat used tubs of water as sensors.

Integrated circuits

An integrated circuit is also called an IC or chip. It is a number of components made and formed into a complete circuit by a special process. Chips are very small and can contain millions of components. Most electronic products now contain chips: computers, calculators, watches, washing machines, etc. Some chips are made for just one purpose, for example, a chip in a musical card that plays a tune (see page 125). Some chips have several uses and others can be programmed to do different jobs.

If enlarged to the size of a book, the circuit of your mobile phone would look like the whole of the A–Z of London, and much more.

■ Musical chips

These chips are contained in a case that looks like a transistor. In fact, the circuit inside contains thousands of components. This is a memory chip that plays back a tune. You simply need to connect it to a battery and a small loudspeaker. This kind of chip is used in greeting cards and in other circuits, such as in an appliance with a recorded voice command.

 More and more sound recording is being done on chips. Tape will soon become a thing of the past.

■ General purpose chips

A very common and useful chip is the 555 timer. With the addition of a few other components, this can be used as a timer or for pulsing something on and off, like a flashing light. The circuit connections are more complicated than for the other circuits, so you will either need to use a prototyping board or make up a printed circuit (see page 129).

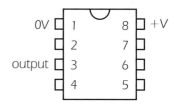

■ A prototyping board will need to be used with a 555 timer

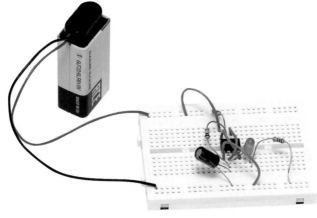

555 timing circuit

This circuit turns something on at a set time after pressing the switch. The length of time depends on the values of the capacitor and resistor. If either of these is a higher value, the time before the LED comes on is longer. A 47 k resistor and 100 µF capacitor will give a time delay of about 5 seconds.

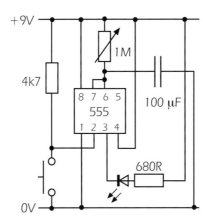

555 pulse circuit

This gives a regular on/off pulse of current. An LED, for example, will turn on for a second, off for a second, on again… and so on. The on and off times are set by the values of the two resistors and the capacitor. The example shown turns on and off once every second.

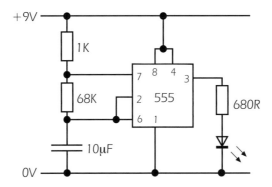

A chip can be as small as the eye of a needle. Most of the chip that you see is the package. This lets humans (with big fingers!) actually handle them and keeps the chip cool because heat is conducted away from it.

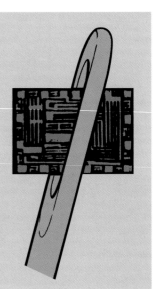

■ Programmable chips

Some chips can now be programmed to do just what you want. The programming is either done using a computer or a special unit. An easy way to use programmable chips is with an IQ board. These boards have a programmable chip and programming switches. You can write a program for the IQ telling it to switch on and off up to three things in a certain order. You can connect a solar motor, buzzer or LED to any of the IQ's outputs.

■ Programmable chip factory

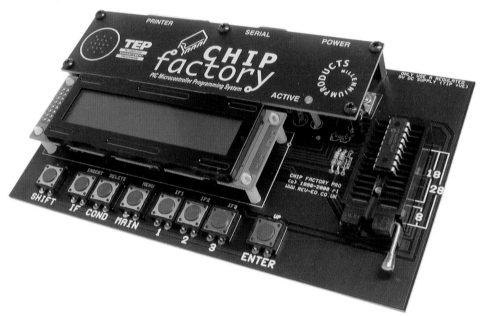

■ IQ controller

Production lines, like those for making car engines, are now controlled by programmable units called PLCs. PLC stands for Programmable Logic Controller. The IQ is a very basic form of a PLC.

Programming IQ

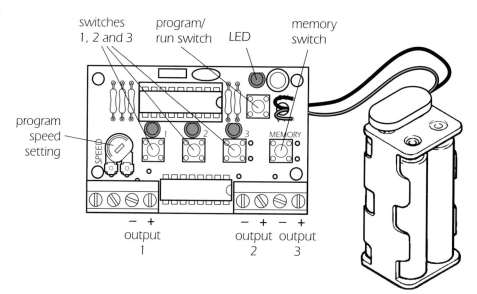

Some IQs have screw-in terminals to allow you to connect components. These are the ones shown here.

Let's assume that we want to turn something on and off connected to output 1.

- First, press the program switch at the top so the LED there is green (green means IQ is ready for programming).
- Then press 'switch 1' and the small LED will come on.
- Press 'memory' and the small LED will flash.
- Press 'switch 1' and the small LED will go off.
- Press 'memory' and the small LED will flash.
- Now press the program switch at the top so the LED there turns red. IQ will now play back your program. The small LED will turn on and off and anything connected to output 1 will also turn on and off.

You can program the IQ with up to 60 steps. You can turn one or two outputs on at each step, for example:

		Output 1	Output 2	Output 3
	1	on	off	off
Lines	**2**	off	on	off
	3			
	4			

You simply need to remember to press 'memory' each time to enter the switch setting into memory. The speed of the program can be adjusted using the small variable resistor on the IQ board.

Making a printed circuit board

Look back at page 99 where we talked about permanent circuits called printed circuits. There are many ways to make a printed circuit board (PCB). The easiest is to start with a board completely covered in a thin layer of copper and to dissolve the unwanted parts with a chemical, leaving only what the circuit needs. The chemical will dissolve anything not covered up. Where copper is wanted, you can cover it up, for example, with a felt-tip pen.

■ **Step 1** Make sure the surface of the copper board is clean

■ **Step 2** Draw the circuit using a permanent marker or PCB pen

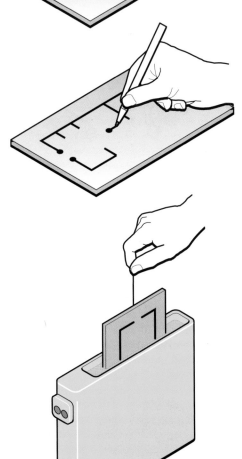

■ **Step 3** Dissolve the unwanted copper in an etching tank

When the bare copper has dissolved, clean the felt-tip ink off what is left.
The components can then be soldered to the copper side of the board, or to the other side with wires and component legs passing through small holes that you can drill in the necessary places (see the pictures on page 99).

Small miracles of electronics

Our modern world depends on electronics. Here are some examples of things that you see everyday. In relevant cases, they are compared with earlier versions to show the progress that has been made.

Radios If you take a transistor radio apart, you will find resistors, capacitors and other special components. Transistor radios are much smaller than early radios because they use chips, which may contain thousands more components.

■ Transistor radio
components

When the BBC began broadcasting in the 1920s, most people used a crystal radioset and headphones. These early radios did not need batteries, just a very long aerial and connection to the earth. The main part of the circuit was a diode, which converted the radio signal into sound. You can still make working crystal radios.

Sound recorders These days sound is stored on chips – in answerphones, voice recorders and music players. A typical sound recorder has a circuit that converts sound into a digital signal (the kind computers understand) and stores it on a chip. The circuit converts this back to sound when needed.

■ Sound recorder
components

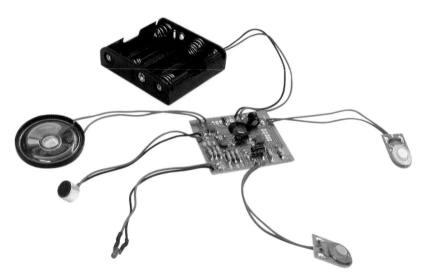

■ A home-made
gramophone

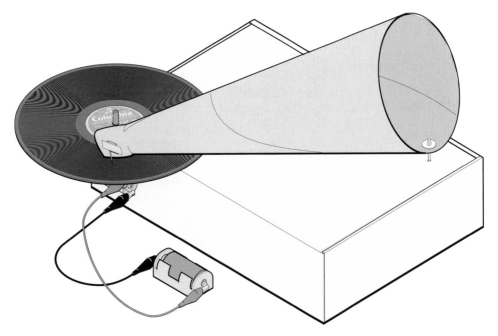

When sound recording began, speech and music were put onto records (cylinders or flat disks) in the form of a wavy groove. The flat records revolved at 78 rpm (revolutions per minute) on a clockwork-powered turntable and the sound, picked up by a needle in the groove, was amplified through a horn. The old name for a record player was a gramophone. You can still make one of these.

Smart batteries We can buy electricity in little 'packets' called batteries. When they are connected to something, chemical changes start up inside the battery, which produce a flow of electric current. Modern batteries produce much more electrical energy for their size than older batteries. A smart battery will tell you if it is flat or not, by using a thermochromic panel.

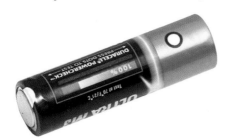

Very early batteries, of some 200 years ago, consisted of pairs of copper and silver metal disks – each pair separated by paper soaked in acid. You can still make one of these with zinc, a 2 pence coin and vinegar (acetic acid) to power a clock or light up an LED.

zinc disc

piece of kitchen towel soaked in vinegar

2 pence piece

3 mm LED

Talking cards and books

If you look carefully at a talking/musical card or book, you will find four things: a switch, a battery, a chip and a speaker. When you open up the card or book the switch connects the battery to the chip. This sends a signal to the speaker. To save cost and space, the chip is sealed under a blob of plastic instead of a case with legs.

CD-ROMs

The CD-ROM has taken over from tape and floppy disks as a means of storing sound, video and computer data. The information on a CD is in the form of a pattern of tiny pits. Millions of these produce a digital information stream to give sound, video or information. The CD is spun at high speed and a laser shines light on the surface. This is reflected back to a sensor that sees the pits. Circuits then process what the sensor picks up. The laser is moved across the CD by special motors, whose movement is minutely controlled by other electronic circuits. Before long, CDs will be out of date and everything will be stored on chips – this will mean no more moving parts to go wrong.

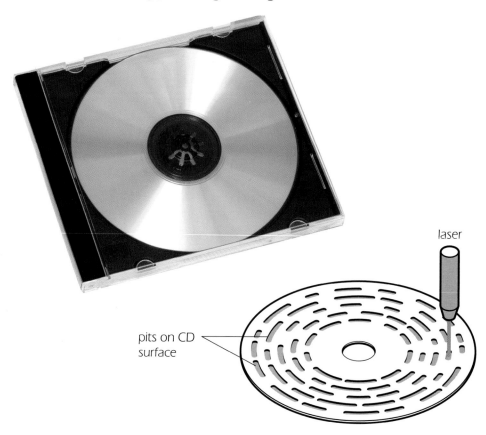

laser

pits on CD surface

Liquid crystal display (LCD) watches

A modern digital watch has a circuit that generates a very fast on/off pulse. This is kept in time by a tiny quartz crystal. The circuit drives a liquid crystal display to show time, date, etc. Because the circuits are based on chips, it does not cost much more to give a really cheap watch lots of extra functions, such as a stopwatch. The accuracy of a cheap watch is now better than a very expensive mechanical one of just a few years ago.

Calculators

Calculators are now the most common and cheapest modern electronic products. If you take one apart, you will find:

- a keyboard for inputting numbers, etc.
- a chip containing up to a million plus components
- a display for showing numbers and sometimes graphics.

The displays of most calculators use liquid crystals, which require very little current to power them. This is why many calculators can now be solar-powered.

■ Solar-powered calculator with an LCD display

The first modern calculators appeared in the early 1970s and used LEDs to display the numbers. They were very expensive, costing up to a hundred times what you might pay today. Before electronic calculators, people used mechanical versions that used gearwheels and other moving parts.

■ Mechanical calculator

Computers People take small computers for granted now, but just a few years ago they existed only as very large mainframes, taking up whole rooms of space. A modern laptop can have more computing power than a machine costing £1 million just 25 years ago! Many people now make their own PCs because they can buy all the parts and just plug them together. The main parts are:

- power supply converting mains voltage to the circuit voltage
- motherboard housing most of the electronics in the form of chips. This includes a central processing chip and memory chips
- disk drive for floppy disks
- drive for reading and burning CD-ROMs
- keyboard for inputting data, and maybe a mouse to operate the functions
- visual display unit (VDU).

Computers are changing shape rapidly because flat screens have taken over from the old TV-type and the electronics are getting smaller all the time. Massive memory is now available on chips, which can be plugged in as opposed to using disk storage.

Contrast all this with the earliest computers, which were mechanical and part electrical. Charles Babbage was an important computer pioneer who almost built a programmable computer using only mechanical parts. Computers developed during the twentieth century used punched cards for inputting and storing data – a method that was used many years earlier to program weaving looms.

■ Early computers took up a lot of space

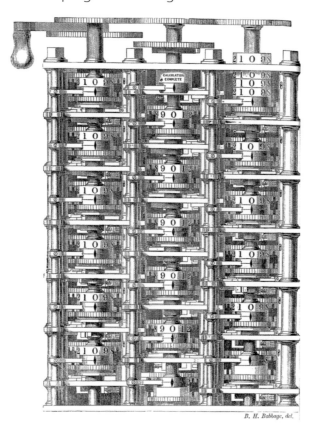

B. H. Babbage, del.

Mobile phones

A mobile phone is a very complicated radio transmitter and receiver. It uses microwave signals (similar to a microwave oven). These signals can be detected with a cheap 'phone flash' circuit.

■ Mobile phone circuits are very complicated

Much of a mobile phone's technology is hidden from view. It is the bigger system that provides you with the service. The signals to and from your mobile are sent and picked up via a network of base stations dotted around towns and in the country. The really clever part is that millions of different calls can be correctly routed and monitored by the system.

Your phone contains:

- a display
- a keyboard
- a processing unit
- transmitter and receiver electronics
- a high-energy battery.

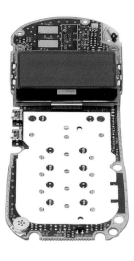

Newer phones are also equipped with cameras so that you can take and send pictures to other people. Many phones give direct access to the internet and are virtually computers in their own right.

Older mobiles were the size of a large briefcase because the electronic circuits and batteries were so much larger.

Remote controllers Most remote controllers for TVs, stereos, etc. use a beam of infra-red radiation. This is similar to light, but is outside our field of vision. Each button pressed sends out a different infra-red signal. This is decoded by a circuit at the receiving end to control volume level, change channels, etc. Many TVs no longer have controls on the set itself. This saves cost. If you lose a remote controller, it is possible to buy an 'all-in-one' replacement, which has codes for most things built into it. Some controllers can actually 'learn' these codes from another controller.

The TEP remote control system uses an 'all-in-one' controller. The receiver, which can turn things on or off, 'thinks' that it is a TV.

■ TEP all-in-one remote control system

Infra-red keys for car security are now common. Each key sends a unique signal to the car to lock or unlock the doors. Unfortunately, these signals can sometimes be picked up and copied.

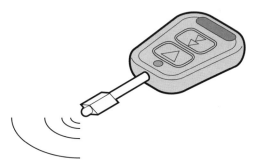

Smart lamps LEDs are gradually replacing older type bulbs for lighting. Very often they use an electronic circuit to turn on and off very quickly. An example is the red rear light used by cyclists. The flashing red light is highly visible, but because it is off for about half the total time, the battery life is much longer. Some LED lights flash so quickly you think they are on all the time, but they are still saving current when all the 'offs' are added together.

■ The cyclist's flashing light is made possible by an LED in the circuit

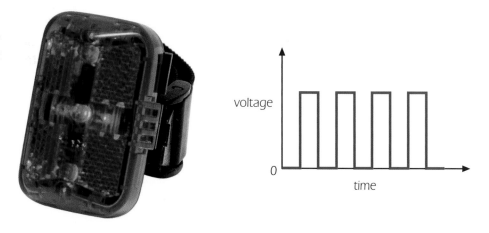

Index

acrylic 4, 32, 41
  shop signs 50
aircraft failures 65
alarm, transistor 116
aluminium metal 29
  anodising 29
  beams 55
  shaping/joining 39
  some uses 48
AND and OR logic 103
automaton 82

Babbage, Charles 135
batteries 94, 110, 131
Baylis, Trevor v, 4
beams 54–8
blow-up structures 63
  make challenge 69
box beams 56–8
brass 30
bridges 62
brief 4
bug toy 84
building collapses 64
buzzers 102–3

cable-stay bridges 62
calculators 133
cam 71
capacitors 112
cardboard engineering 77–8
CD-ROMs 132
chipboard 35
circuits 93, 97–9
clocks 4
clockwork radio 4, 6
clockwork toys 7
composites (material) 26
compressive force 52
computer drawings 17
computer numerically
    controlled (CNC)
    machines 23, 43
computer-aided design (CAD)
    17–19
computer-aided machining
    (CAM) 23–4
computers 134–5
conductors and insulators 94
construction kits 77
copper 30
cranks 71, 75
crash helmet 28
current (electric) flow 94
  measurement 95

design and make challenges
    43–7, 68–9, 81–4
design and technology 1–7
door bells 103
drawings 9–19
drink cans 51

Eden Project, Cornwall 60
Edison, Thomas 5
electronic components 93
electronic measurement 95–6
electronics in control 60–137
electrons 94

field effect transistors (FET)
    119–20
foamalux board 34
forces and structures 52–3
frames, as structures 58–60
Fuller, Buckminster 60
fuse tester 109

games with transistors
    117–18
gearboxes 71, 74
gears 71
geodesic frames 60
glow-in-the-dark materials 37
glues and fastening 21, 40,
    42

hands-on/off making 38–43
helping hand, making 83

ideas 8–25
inflatable structures 63
infra-red car keys 137
insulation/insulators 28, 94
integrated circuits (ICs or
    chips) 124–8
IQ boards 127–8

kinetic art machine 84

laminated wood 42
laminating 77
lamps, filament 102
latching switches 100
LCDs (liquid crystal displays)
    133
LDR (light-dependent resistor)
    108, 117
LEDs (light-emitting diodes)
    104–5, 109
lever 72
light dimmers 110
light meter 111
linkages 72, 75
London Eye 61

mat switches 117
materials 26–50
  shaping materials 38–43
  small miracles with 48–50
MDF (medium density
    fibreboard) 35
measurement, electrical 95–6
mechanisms 70–3
  design and make
    challenges 81–4

making mechanisms 77–80
mechanical parts 74–5
small mechanical miracles
    92
membrane panel switches
    101
metal rods 80
metal sheet 80
metals 29–31
  shaping 39
Millennium bridge 67
Millennium Dome 62
mirrors, plastic 43
mobile phones 135–6
models/modelling 20–4
  fastening methods 21
moisture detector 105, 116
money box, electronic 113
multimeters 96
musical chips 125

orthographic drawings 16

perspective 10–12
pewter 31
photochromic pigment 37
pin block circuits 98
plastic materials 32–4
plastic sheet 40–1, 79
plywood 35
polymorph 34, 79
polypropylene 7, 33, 49
polystyrene 33, 40, 79
polythene 32
press button switches 100
printed circuit boards 129
problem prevention 66–7
programmable chips 127–8
prototyping board circuits 99
pulley 72

radios 130
rapid prototyping (RP)
    machines 24
remote controllers 136–7
resistance measurement 96
resistors 107–8
  light-dependent (LDR) 108,
    117
  variable 108
robot challenge 85–91
rocker switches 100
roof failures 65

sensors, with thermistors 123
shape memory alloy (SMA)
    36
shear force 53
sheet plastics 40–1
shelf failures 65
silver 30, 50
slide switches 100
smart batteries 131

smart materials 36–7
  smart colours 37
  smart film 26
  smart grease 73
  smart wire (SMA wire) 36
  smartlink 73, 80
softlink tubing 73
solar-powered torch 113
sound recorders 130–1
spring board circuits 99
springs 73, 75
steel 29
strength of materials 27
structures 51–69
  problem prevention 66–7
  see also forces and
    structures
suspension bridges 62
switches 100–2, 117, 122

talking cards and books 132
technology see design and
    technology
Technology Enhancement
    Programme (TEP)
  modelling board 34
  remote control system
    136–7
  see also Introduction
telegraph signalling 106
tensile force 52
terminal block circuits 98
thermistors 109, 111
thermochromic film/pigment
    36–7
thermometer 111
thyristors 121–3
tilt switches 122
timers 116, 125–6
  transistor 116
  type 555 chip 125–6
titanium 31
  jewellery 49
toggle switches 100
transistors 114–15
  circuits with 116–17
  games with 117–18
  see also field effect
    transistors (FET)
trembler switches 122
triangular frames 59
trusses 58

voltage measurement 95

watches, liquid crystal 133
widget 83
wiggly wire game 113, 118
wire/cable structures 61–3
wood/wood products 27, 35
  cutting/joining 42
  laminated wood 42
  structures 49